To the

Jack in the Box Family!

Dan Coughlin

THE *MANAGEMENT* **500**

A High-Octane Formula for Business Success

DAN COUGHLIN

AMACOM

AMERICAN MANAGEMENT ASSOCIATION

New York • Atlanta • Brussels • Chicago • Mexico City • San Francisco •
Shanghai • Tokyo • Toronto • Washington, D.C.

Special discounts on bulk quantities of AMACOM books are
available to corporations, professional associations, and other
organizations. For details, contact Special Sales Department,
AMACOM, a division of American Management Association,
1601 Broadway, New York, NY 10019.
Tel: 212-903-8316. Fax: 212-903-8083.
E-mail: specialsls@amanet.org
Website: www.amacombooks.org/go/specialsales
To view all AMACOM titles go to: www.amacombooks.org

This publication is designed to provide accurate and authoritative
information in regard to the subject matter covered. It is sold with the
understanding that the publisher is not engaged in rendering legal,
accounting, or other professional service. If legal advice or other expert
assistance is required, the services of a competent professional person
should be sought.

Library of Congress Cataloging-in-Publication Data

Coughlin, Dan
    The management 500 : a high-octane formula for business success / Dan Coughlin.
       p.   cm.
    Includes bibliographical references and index.
    ISBN-13: 978-0-8144-1423-1
    ISBN-10: 0-8144-1423-0
    1. Management.   2. Success in business.   3. Organizational effectiveness.   4. Business
enterprises.   I. Title.   II. Title: Management five hundred.

HD31.C64493   2009
658.4'09—dc22

                                                                                              2008046442

Printing number

10   9   8   7   6   5   4   3   2

To **MOM** and **DAD,**
who taught Kevin, Cathy, Jim, Mick, Mary Eileen, and me
how to live our lives with precision. Your impact will sustain itself
for many lifetimes.

Mom and Dad, I love you.

THANK YOU for everything you have done for me.

CONTENTS

FOREWORD

I find great comfort in listening to great stories and I bet you do too.

Chances are that your favorite teachers and professors were gifted storytellers and the same is probably true of your best friends, favorite family members, and other memorable characters in your life. Unfortunately, great stories and storytellers are rare.

A great story has to have a beginning that draws listeners in and makes them want to listen, vivid detail in the telling that allows listeners to feel and live the story being told, and a resounding finish that leaves an indelible life lesson or moral having been learned. I believe that Dan Coughlin is one of America's best new business storytellers and authors.

I also admire great thinkers, and with this book Coughlin distinguishes himself as one of the nation's best contemporary business thinkers. Recent events in worldwide financial markets have proved again that the old rules of achieving and maintaining success are no longer valid. The meltdown has also exposed most of the people who pretended to have all the answers and the right way of doing things as greedy little poseurs.

Dan Coughlin's new book about winning the business race and sustaining profitable business growth is filled with great new stories and new lessons that will serve you well.

I hear from scores of aspiring business authors and speakers asking for advice and guidance on their careers. Being a firm believer in karma, I'm always pleased to try and help out. A few years ago Dan came to me asking for some advice and I was immediately struck by the big differences between him and so many others who reach out to me.

Dan came to our first meeting with a long list of written questions but before he got to ask them I asked him to spend a few minutes telling me about himself. He took a deep breath, put his list down, and said, "I'm married to a woman I love more than the day I married her, and I have two children who along with my wife are the most important things in my life." I decided I liked him immediately.

Dan Coughlin is the real deal. His head and heart are in the right place and his books are written for people who want to achieve success in business but still have time to enjoy the *really* important things in life. Dan knows the profound impact a teacher can have on helping others achieve their full potential and writes books to help others become all they dream about being and achieving.

None of us—and I place myself at the top of the list—are as good as we think we are and we must constantly strive to become better at what we do. *The Management 500: A High-Octane Formula for Business Success* will become an invaluable part of your management and leadership arsenal.

Jason Jennings
Tiburon, California
2009

ACKNOWLEDGMENTS

First and foremost, I want to say thank you to my literary agent, Jeff Herman. This is our third book together and each project has been more exciting than the one before it.

Second, I want to thank Ellen Kadin and the marvelous team at AMACOM for all of their support on this book. You did a beautiful job in helping me to hone and deliver my message. I also want to thank Jill Wettstein, my graphic artist, who crafted the graphic visuals for this book.

Third, thanks to Dave Pelliccioni at Toyota Financial Services; Ed Laukes, Les Unger, Diana DeJoseph, and Kym Strong at Toyota Motorsports; Lee White at Toyota Racing Development; and Geoff Smith and Torrey Galida at Roush Fenway Racing for helping me to understand the inner workings of NASCAR and the intricate relationships between racing teams, owners, drivers, fans, and sponsors.

Fourth, thank you to my wonderful parents, Gene and Laura Coughlin, and my terrific siblings, Kevin, Cathy, Jim, Mick, and Mary Eileen, who have been listening to all my crazy dreams for all of these years.

Fifth, thanks very, very much to my very, very patient family: my wife, Barb, and our children, Sarah and Ben. You three are truly awesome, and I appreciate you and love you very, very much.

INTRODUCTION

The Management 500 is the business manager's ultimate challenge.

The Management 500 is the real-world race for people who run a business or manage a profit center to generate significant and sustainable profitable growth for three consecutive years. It's fairly easy for a manager to achieve profitable growth for one year. The far greater challenge is to generate significant profitable growth year after year after year for three consecutive years.

The history of professional auto racing is filled with intriguing events, people, and lessons for the modern business manager to learn from. In a Formula 1 Grand Prix, NASCAR Sprint Cup Series,[1] or IndyCar Series race anywhere from twenty to forty-three of the world's fastest drivers in the world's fastest cars compete for approximately three hours with the expectation of going as fast and as smart as possible. The driver and his or her team are responsible for continually finding ways to make their car move with greater speed and accuracy and to sustain that performance over an extended period of time.

I've always admired the power and speed of professional auto racing, but I didn't understand the nuances, strategies, and required commitments until I began my research for this book. The farther I threw myself into studying individuals, cars, and organizations that make up the world of professional auto racing, the more clearly the management insights came to me.

From Enzo Ferrari to Jimmie Johnson, from McLaren Formula 1

Racing Team to Toyota Racing Development, from the Indianapolis 500 to the Daytona 500, and from BMW to Chevrolet, I've stepped into this vast and fast universe to see what ideas the modern business manager can extract from professional auto racing and use in his or her day job. The answer, it turns out, is a lot.

In addition to all the books on car racing that I've listed in the notes at the end of this book, I taped the Formula 1 French Grand Prix, Formula 1 German Grand Prix, and the Indianapolis 500, where I was able to see over and over again how the drivers went into the turns and passed one another. However, a few pieces of research stand out as real highlights.

First, I found a rare original edition copy of Enzo Ferrari's autobiography. This book was extremely motivating and insightful. Written in 1963, it helped to explain the reasons for the amazing long-term success of the Ferrari brand.

Second, I had the opportunity to interview Lee White, the president of Toyota Racing Development, USA. Lee's passion and sense of purpose was so remarkable that it reminded me of what I learned from Enzo Ferrari. I then spoke with Ed Laukes, the executive who oversees all of Toyota Motorsports in the United States, and he gave me some very helpful insights into how NASCAR strengthens the brands of car manufacturers, and, more importantly, he shared his thoughts on how any business in any industry can strengthen its brand.

Third, I interviewed Geoff Smith, the president of Roush Fenway Racing, which in recent years has become one of the top racing organizations in NASCAR. He shared with me powerful insights on how to compete successfully and strengthen not only your organization's brand but also the brands of your sponsors.

However, the most interesting day of my research was attending the 2008 NASCAR Sprint Cup Series LifeLock.com 400 at the Chicagoland Speedway. The race began at 7PM, and I drove into the parking lot at 11 AM, eight hours before the action started. Or so I thought. It turns out that I was attending my first NASCAR race as a fan on the exact fiftieth anniversary of Richard Petty's first NASCAR race as a driver, which was on July 12, 1958.

A NASCAR race is so much more than just a car race. It's a Super Bowl event. There were 75,000 people there, and I estimate there were at least 20,000 people tailgating at 11 AM. I repeat this was *eight* hours before the race started. It's a giant carnival, with actual old-fashioned barkers yelling out that they had free offers inside their tents. It's a giant concert with singers and entertainers on stage all day. It's a massive outdoor mall with over 100 booths selling caps, shirts, buttons, miniature cars, giant corn dogs—and even some lemonade stands.

A NASCAR event attracts every conceivable brand name product. I walked through the largest Abraham Lincoln museum I'd ever been in outside of Washington, D.C., and Springfield, Illinois, and it was on wheels. I saw a display of dozens of the largest and most magnificent televisions I had ever seen. However, the strongest brands there were the racecar drivers themselves. People of all ages wore shirts with the faces and numbers of their favorite drivers.

There are forty-three drivers who compete at each NASCAR Sprint Cup Series race and there are thirty-six such races each year. This is a traveling circus that is bigger than any circus I had ever witnessed. And then there's the race itself. You haven't heard LOOOUUUDDDD until you've heard a NASCAR race. If you haven't been to a race, then watching it on television doesn't explain the speed well either. These cars were within a few inches of each other going at 160 mph and jumping from high to low on the turns in the track.

The whole day pulsated with lessons both inside and outside the track on branding, innovation, teamwork, strategy, execution, planning, problem solving, winning, dealing with change, and preparation. It was an amazing experience.

Details win races. They also lose them. It comes down to selection and execution.

In car racing a driver has to decide when to push forward and when to take a pit stop. He or she has to make a constant series of instantaneous decisions to not only stay in the race but to stay in one piece. The weeks and months leading up to a major race consist of detailed preparations from team owners, car designers, team managers, crew chiefs, crew members, and the drivers themselves. Projects include establishing a strategy for the race, building effective teamwork between the driver and the pit crew, and designing and building and fine-tuning the car itself. Every detail is important.

The modern business manager has to do exactly the same thing. How does a business manager accelerate profitable growth in a sustainable way for three straight years? Whether a manager runs a multibillion-dollar corporation or a hundred-thousand-dollar profit center, that's the challenge he or she faces. The manager and his or her team have to achieve desired results quickly and improve performance month after month. This book provides insights from the world of professional auto racing that can be applied to win that business race.

Unlike a professional car race that lasts for three hours give or take a little, the Management 500 lasts for three years. You have the next three years, assuming the wheels don't fall off the car, to steadily generate greater levels of profit for your organization and to do it in a way that is sustainable for the long term.

You're not competing with other businesses or to be the best in your industry or to generate the most revenues or to have the most employees. You're racing against the clock. You have to produce profitable growth this year, next year, and the year after that. That's the event you're competing in. At the end of three years, you can prepare for the next three-year race.

You may very well have to redefine the performance business you're in, and you may find that smaller is better, and more profitable. Or you may have to increase your investments, add more employees, and increase your marketing.

The Management 500 is not the rat race so many of us heard about growing up. Instead it's an exciting and challenging race that will cause you to grow personally and professionally. It will cause you to look inward and understand yourself better, and look outward to better understand your boss, peers, employees, suppliers, and, most important, customers. There will always be a sense of urgency, whether the short-term results are good or poor. And that sense of urgency will bring out the best in you. It will be a better best than you ever thought possible.

Managers today not only need to be better prepared than ever before, but they also have to deal with an unprecedented rate of change in digital technology, consumer trends, globalization, communication, and transportation. Team members who once sat in the same conference room are now spread across continents and communicate via webcasts, podcasts, instant messaging, and e-mail. Outsourcing has become so prevalent that 30 percent or more of an organization may be there only on a temporary basis.

As a manager you need to develop your skills and insights to generate sustainable, profitable growth, but if you're like most managers you only have a few minutes a day to invest in your own development. Many times it may feel as though you are buzzing around a track with competitors zooming all around you. Even if you want to work all day every day, you will find out very quickly that burnout is a real issue. Pit stops are necessities to rejuvenate your mind and your energy in order to drive results to a higher and more sustainable level.

This book is designed for the busy manager who wants to compete and win in the highly competitive and fast-paced business world in which we live. It was created to provide you with practical insights you can read in a few minutes and then reflect on to find ways to accelerate the achievement of your most important desired business outcomes.

Over the past eleven years, I've worked with large and mid-size companies to improve their business momentum. One of my main activities has been to work closely with the executives and managers who ran the business or managed the profit center. I've served as a management consultant for more than 130 executives and managers in more than thirty industries. Some of these individuals worked in huge corporations like Toyota, McDonald's, Marriott, and Coca-Cola. Many others worked in mid-size organizations, including CEOs and business owners.

I've invested more than 3,000 hours on site at these companies observing the managers in the flow of their normal work-day activities. I sat in large, small, and private meetings with these individuals. I observed them as they dealt with issues related to strategy, planning, execution, talent management, personal effectiveness, priority management, leadership, teamwork, innovation, and branding. At the end of each visit we discussed my observations.

My goal with these managers was to co-create simple, practical processes that they could take with them into their work situations to try to improve their performance. A manager would try a process out, and then we would discuss how it worked in the reality of a business situation. Then we worked to refine the process to make it more useful in a practical way.

This book provides a few dozen of these proven practical processes from real-world business situations that you can use to improve the sustainable achievement of your most important desired business outcomes. As you go through the various processes, I have two thoughts of encouragement for you: embrace simplicity and avoid process creep.

It's been my experience that really smart, really hardworking, and really dedicated managers subconsciously want things to be really complicated because if a process is really complex then it feels more like work. Many times I've seen managers take a simple process that is working well and producing very good results and make it much more complicated in the hopes of achieving amazing results. It doesn't usually work out that way. The complicated process tends to bog people down and waste time. This is what I call process creep.

I encourage you to avoid process creep like the plague and to see that a simple process is much more powerful than a complicated process because you can implement a simple process faster, teach it to others faster, and customize it to your situation faster. The practical processes in this book are two to seven steps long. They are clear and simple. Don't be fooled by their simplicity.

If you want to win the race for sustainable, profitable growth, the key is to move quickly in ways that generate sustainable improvement in key results. Embracing simplicity will increase the speed with which you achieve better results.

Remember also to take regular breaks. If you're looking for me to say you have to work 24/7/365 in order to accelerate sustainable, profitable growth, you've come to the wrong person. I want you to focus your efforts and the efforts of your organization within reasonable time boundaries each week and to do so over the next three years. I also very much want you to have a life outside of work. Actually, I believe your non-work life will help the quality of your work a great deal.

The purpose of this book is to be a resource you can turn to during the calm stretches and the turbulent times in the race ahead. Turn to it often, not for inspiration, but for practical ideas you can use right away to accelerate to victory.

Michael Schumacher is arguably the greatest race car driver in Formula 1 Grand Prix history. He won seven Formula 1 Grand Prix World Championships, which is two more than the next closest competitor, and he won five of them in succession from 2000–2004. However, in his very first Grand Prix race, he went way too fast at the start of the race, his car broke down, and he was done after a few seconds.

According to Christopher Hilton, author of *Michael Schumacher: The Whole Story*, Schumacher had to learn a very important skill: to drive fast slowly.[2] He needed to slow down his thoughts so he could drive at nearly 200 mph while passing other drivers, increasing his lead, and thinking through his upcoming decisions. At his peak, Schumacher calmly held conversations with his crew chief while maneuvering at breakneck speeds. He always looked refreshed at the end of his races rather than exhausted.

As you go through the ideas in this book, I encourage you to drive fast slowly. Slow your life as a manager down a bit and think through your answers to the questions I pose. The questions take just a few minutes to answer, but they do require you to slow down and answer them thoughtfully in order to go faster toward the achievement of sustainable, profitable growth.

You'll quickly notice the book is laid out in the form of a race around the business track. If you're a fan of auto racing, you'll also quickly notice that the book is not laid out in the exact same fashion as an actual race. I begin with thoughts on preparing yourself for long-term success as a manager and later talk about assembling a team and developing a strategy. In an actual auto race you would first assemble a team and later on would prepare for a given race. Such slight differences aside, I believe you will find the history of professional auto racing to be an intriguing place to find powerful management insights.

Dan Coughlin
Fenton, MO
March 2009

THE MANAGEMENT *500*

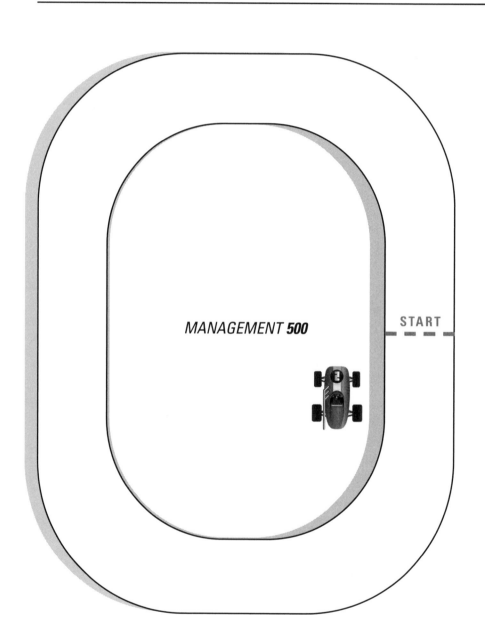

CHAPTER ONE

MANAGEMENT *500*

START

PREPARE WITH
PRECISION

*"*I am mainly interested in promoting new developments. I should like to put something new into my cars every morning—an inclination that terrifies my staff. Were my wishes in this respect to be indulged, there would be no production of standard models at all, but only a succession of prototypes.[1]*"*
   —Enzo Ferrari

Precision matters.

Enzo Ferrari had a greater impact on the world of professional auto racing than almost any other person in history. After racing cars and serving as a mechanic for Alfa on the highly successful Alfa Romeos in the 1920s and 1930s, he started his own business. In 1946, at the age of forty-eight, he concentrated all of his efforts on designing and building his own car, which bore his name.[2]

Over the next six plus decades, the name Ferrari has become synonymous with extraordinary speed—and with winning. His cars participated in the first Formula 1 Grand Prix World Championship in 1950, and over the next 60 years Enzo Ferrari and his successors won championships in 1952, 1953, 1956, 1958, 1961, 1964, 1975, 1977, 1979, 2000–2004, and 2007. I would call that sustained greatness.

Enzo Ferrari's passion was precision. He wanted every part of his organization dedicated to increasing precision in the execution of every detail. He wrote, "All odds and ends of technical information are of interest to builders of racing cars, because a secondary detail can sometimes give a clever engineer a lead to something much more important. The heat of a spark plug, the type of fuel used, the kind of steel employed for the valves, the address of this or that supplier, together with an infinity of other details, are all useful."[3]

His famous emblem of a prancing horse on a yellow shield became a symbol of true greatness in winning through precision. Every year the Ferrari drivers attempt to tame the prancing horse by winning the Formula 1 Grand Prix World Championship. Every time Ferrari wins, people throughout Italy cheer one of their most famous sons. Enzo Ferrari created one of the world's greatest brands.[4]

Because Enzo Ferrari consistently prepared his team to win the race in front of them, he gained legendary status. He was named as an example of Italian genius in the book, *Sprezzatura: 50 Ways Italian Genius Shaped the World*, along with Julius Ceasar, Leonardo da Vinci, and Michelangelo.[5]

For you, as a business manager, precision also matters. The power of precision is available to every manager. Striving for precision is the most effective way for you to succeed as a manager over the long term.

THE NOBLE CALLING TO BE A PRECISIONIST

In *The Pocket Webster School & Office Dictionary*, the word "precision" means demanding exactness. Therefore, I'm defining a precisionist as a person who has mastered the art of demanding exactness. The precisionist operates among the very best performers in the world within a given area of focus and constantly works to improve his or her performance.

When customers and employers are hit hard in the wallet they become extraordinarily discerning about where they place their dollars. Customers become highly selective in terms of what they invest in. Employers develop a laser focus about only going after the type of managers they absolutely need and seeking out only the best of the best within that target.

If you want to fall into that extremely small slice of managers who are always in demand, then I encourage you to be a precisionist. The business race for sustainable, profitable growth is too difficult to win for you to be anything less than a precisionist as a manager.

Demanding exactness from yourself and from other people doesn't mean you have to be a jerk or a dictator. It means you have to have a very clear idea of exactly what you expect in terms of performance from yourself and from other people. Then you have to demand nothing less than for everyone to work together toward that exact expectation.

Examples of Precisionists

While precisionists are extraordinary, examples of precisionists are abundant.

Truth be told, I'm not a golf fan. Watching men and women hit a little white ball into a hole for four days is not my idea of a good time, except when Tiger Woods plays. Then I pile up the pillows and watch the master at work. What I'm really watching is not golf, but rather a precisionist applying his craft.

All Tiger Woods does is improve. He searches for ways to become more precise in the application of his craft. People call him superhuman, but the truth is we can all get better at what we do. That's right. We *all* have the capacity to be the Tiger Woods within a given area of focus. The keys are . . . , well, I'll talk more about that in a little while.

Eric Clapton is the only three-time inductee into the Rock and Roll Hall of Fame. In 1964, his first full year as a professional musician with the Yardbirds, he played in over 200 gigs. However, he felt that to become a precisionist, a musician needed to keep performing. In his book, *Clapton: The Autobiography*, he wrote, "To fully develop your craft you need to interact with other people."[6]

Practice is wonderful, but it won't force you to take your skills to the next level. Even though he had been on the road performing since the age of nineteen, he still felt throughout his career that it was important to get back in front of a live audience in order to improve his performance.

If you want to be a better leader, jump in and lead, even if it means volunteering to be on an unpaid committee. If you want to achieve precision as a manager, then take on the responsibility to manage a key profit center. You can't practice your way to become a precisionist as a manager. You have to jump in and take on real challenges.

Recently I drove home from my sister's house. On the way I was stopped by a man holding a "Stop/Slow" sign. At first I thought, "How can a person do that job day after day? Isn't that terribly boring?" And then it dawned on me the extreme importance of his work and the work of the crew repaving the road. If he lacked precision, cars would run into each other, and if the crew lacked precision, they would end up creating a road that was uneven. Precisionists are needed in every industry and every walk of life. They are the ones who stand out in the crowd and establish a higher standard for what is possible.

Ron Dennis, the long-time head of the McLaren Formula 1 Racing Team, personified the art of demanding exactness. Prior to Dennis's joining McLaren in September 1980, they had won two Formula 1 Grand Prix World Championships, in 1974 and 1976. His first move was to hire John Barnard to be his Formula 1 car designer. As Alan Henry describes in his book, *McLaren Formula 1 Racing Team*, "Dennis's enthusiasm for engineering excellence was tempered by a degree of business savvy. He was interested in Formula 1, but not at any price. If he was going to do it, he would do it properly."[7]

Dennis built a culture that believed perfection was just good enough. From 1984–1999, the McLaren Formula 1 Racing Team won the Formula 1 Grand Prix World Championship nine times with four different drivers: Niki Lauda, Alain Prost, Ayrton Senna, and Mika Hakkinen.

Ron Dennis said, "I have a belief that everything is important in life and everything is important when you are trying to achieve high levels of success in any business—certainly in Formula 1. I believe that at all times you should have the best—or at least try to have the best. This is not simply about money, it is mainly about commitment. We try to inspire it into the very fiber of everyone's approach to their work for the team."[8]

The challenge we all face is not in finding examples of precisionists, but rather in becoming a precisionist. And why does becoming a precisionist remain such a great challenge? Well, we get a little busy with our lives and before we know it today is over with and we're on to tomorrow, and we haven't exactly made very much progress in becoming more precise in what we're doing. In other words, the busyness of life takes over our best intentions until bedtime beckons us.

I encourage you to step off the train of constant activity, invest time in thinking through what you're doing as you go about managing, and make real progress toward becoming more of a true precisionist as a manager.

The Process for Becoming a Precisionist as a Manager

1.   Select great management performance as your umbrella.

2.   Maintain a high degree of focus for at least fourteen years.

3.   Leverage technology.

Select Great Management Performance as Your Umbrella

Your umbrella is the area of focus you've decided to achieve precision within. This is the area you're committing to operating within over the long term.

Walt Disney's umbrella was family entertainment. Under any umbrella there is plenty of room to maneuver and create. Walt Disney made family films and television shows, he created theme parks, he licensed products, and he started amazingly popular clubs like The Mickey Mouse Club. Having a single area of focus isn't a limiting factor. It's actually a freeing factor. It allows you to operate with extraordinary freedom within a given umbrella and enhance the synergy between everything you do.

Operating under the umbrella of great management performance allows you the freedom to improve your impact in a variety of meaningful areas ranging from establishing a strategy to assembling a true team to executing a plan to building a great brand for your organization.

Maintain a High Degree of Focus for at Least Fourteen Years

Patience is a business driver.

If there's one lesson I've learned in studying successful performers and organizations over the past twenty years, it's that sustained patience leads to extraordinary results. Success takes time. Many of the greatest precisionists in history invested well over a decade in honing their craft.

Michael Schumacher said, "People keep asking me how it is I can come into Formula 1 and establish myself so quickly near the top level and for me there is a simple answer: experience. Although I am very young compared to some of the other drivers I have spent a long time in motorsport, nineteen years altogether, and I have had really good preparation for the job."[9] He had started driving karts at the age of four years old in 1973 and he didn't become a Formula 1 driver until 1991. By the age of twenty-two he was a very, very experienced driver.

The actor/comedian Steve Martin invested fourteen years, from 1963–1977, before he became a national phenomenon as the most popular stand-up comic in history.

In his book, *Born Standing Up: A Comic's Life*, he referred to the beginning of his journey when he wrote, "I was enamored of the rhythmic poetry of e.e. cummings, and a tantalizing quote from one of his recorded lectures stayed in my head. When asked why he became a poet, he said, 'Like the burlesque comedian, I am abnormally fond of that precision which creates movement.' The line, with its intriguing reference to comedy, was enigmatic, and it took me ten years to work out its meaning."[10] For fourteen years Steve Martin worked to hone the precision of his act to the point that people fell on the ground laughing even though he told no punch lines.

At age nineteen in 1973, Oprah Winfrey began to work for

WLAC-TV in Nashville. At twenty-two, she became a reporter and co-anchor at WJZ-TV in Baltimore, and at twenty-four she began hosting talk shows at WJZ-TV. In 1986, she was the host of the number-one ranked nationally syndicated television talk show, *The Oprah Winfrey Show*. Over the course of fourteen years, Oprah Winfrey developed her precision as an interviewer and has sustained her greatness for more than twenty years.[11]

Tiger Woods began playing competitive golf at age seven and won his first major golf tournament in 1997 at age twenty-one by winning the Masters Golf Tournament. By the time he walked away with that first green jacket he had already invested fourteen years in honing his performance. He went on to win the 1999, 2000, 2006, and 2007 U.S. PGA title; 2000, 2002, and 2008 U.S. Open; the 2000, 2005, and 2006 British Open; and the Masters in 2001, 2002, and 2005. He is on target to break Jack Nicklaus's all-time record of winning eighteen major golf tournaments.

Walt Disney began making animated short films in 1921 at the age of nineteen and made the world's first full-length animated film, *Snow White and the Seven Dwarfs*, in 1937 just before he turned thirty-six.

Neal Gabler, author of *Walt Disney: The Triumph of the American Imagination*, described the precision of Disney's effort in the following way: "Walt was moving so incrementally, scene by scene, line by line, even word by word, that by the spring of 1935 he had yet to name all the dwarfs or characterize them, much less finalize the script. If there was any possibility to a scene, he seemed determined not to overlook it. *Snow White* would not be rushed, even if that meant disregarding the original schedule. It would percolate for as long as it took the film to brew."[12]

Harrison Ford started acting in 1963 at the age of twenty-one. He received his first starring role in *Star Wars* in 1977, although at the time a lot of people doubted whether *Star Wars* would attract any attention at all. He then got the lead role in *Raiders of the Lost Ark* as Indiana Jones at age thirty-eight. Ford said, "All I would tell people is to hold on to what is individual about themselves. Not to allow their ambition for success to cause them to try and imitate the success of others. You've got to find it on your own terms."[13]

While he was struggling to make a living as an actor, Harrison Ford was a full-time carpenter for six years. Biographer Robert Sellers wrote:

> When Ford started out in Hollywood he recognized that the best way to pursue acting was not to imitate someone else's success, but develop what was particular about himself. Ford was to teach himself how to act precisely the same way he taught himself carpentry. To him they are crafts and his approach to both is almost entirely technical. Ford sees building a character as no different than turning a stack of timber into a bookshelf or a cupboard. It is a question of submitting oneself to the logic of the craft, and if one starts with a firm foundation, every subsequent step becomes part of that logical process.[14]

Joe Gibbs was an assistant college and professional coach for fifteen years, not counting his time as a graduate assistant, before he became a head NFL coach. Imagine waiting that long for your first big shot. However, Gibbs didn't just put in the time. He honed his craft during those fifteen years. Over the next eleven years he won the Super Bowl three times, in 1983, 1988, and 1992. He then repeated this pattern as the owner of Joe Gibbs Racing, which he founded in 1992. In his first eight seasons he never won a championship. He then won the NASCAR Winston Cup, later named the Nextel Cup, in 2000, 2002, and 2005. Precisionists constantly search to improve the exactness of what it takes to win, and that approach can be applied in multiple industries, as Joe Gibbs has proven.

If you want to be a precisionist as a manager, remain committed to constantly improving within the umbrella of great management performance for at least fourteen years. You might be wondering how pursuing precision can help you achieve a three-year goal like the Management 500 if it takes at least fourteen years to become a precisionist.

Here's how it works. The moment you commit yourself to a specific umbrella, a specific area of focus, you begin to attract people and opportunities to you that will help you hone your craft within that arena. In doing so, you become more attractive to other people. They know what you are focused on and they admire you for pursuing excellence in that field. They may not say that to you, but that's what happens.

When you select the umbrella of great management performance, you probably won't be a world-class manager right away, and that's OK. You are on your way to becoming a precisionist in a field that you have passion for and that sense of adventure is worth a great deal. It's the same type of precision and adventure that the world's greatest racecar drivers pursue.

Leverage Technology

I used to think that technology meant computers, software, and electronics. I wasn't even close. In *The Pocket Webster School & Office Dictionary*, the definition of *technology* is "science used in a practical way." The definition of *science* is "systemized knowledge obtained by study, observation, and experiment." Consequently, technology means systemized knowledge obtained by study, observation, and experiment that is used in a practical way. I *love* that definition. That's exactly what precisionists do.

Tiger Woods is a student of golf: the history of golf, the great players from the past, and the different holes on the different courses. He experiments with different types of shots until he's able to use them in a practical way during a professional golf tournament.

Walt Disney constantly observed people and experimented with different ways to tell entertaining stories in practical ways. He was one of the first to use color in films, he embraced television when others ran away from it, and he created the first ever theme park.

Enzo Ferrari constantly searched for better ways to make his cars go faster and to sustain their performance at incredibly high levels over long periods of time.

You have the ability to leverage technology in order to increase the exactness with which you and your employees perform. The key is to constantly study, observe, and experiment within the umbrella of great management performance, and then use what you learn in practical ways that add value to your employees, customers, suppliers, and colleagues.

THE MEASURES OF A MANAGER'S SUCCESS

There are two measures of your success as a manager, as represented in Figure 1.1.

The first measure consists of your actual business results such as top-line sales, bottom-line profits, the attraction and retention of great customers, and the attraction and retention and development of great employees. Business results are tangible and organizational. They are real, they exist outside of you where everyone can see them, and they are about what your organization has achieved rather than what activities you have done.

The second measure of your success as a manager is your self-confidence. In a business sense, self-confidence is the degree to which you believe you're going to succeed in guiding your organization to

FIGURE 1.1 *Success as a Business Manager*

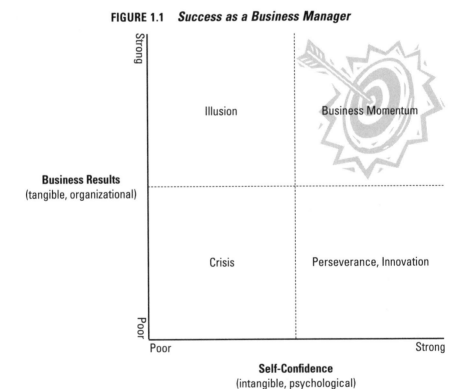

even greater success in the future. Self-confidence is intangible and psychological. You can't measure it and no one can see it. It exists within your mind.

As you can see in Figure 1.1, when a manager has poor self-confidence and poor business results, he faces a crisis. He's wondering if he's the right person for the job, and the people in his organization are wondering if he's the right person for the job.

When a manager has poor self-confidence and strong business results, she feels it's an illusion. I've had many managers say to me, "The reasons I'm getting great results are the market conditions are so good and I inherited a great long-term customer who has sustained our profits. However, I personally am not part of the reason why we're successful, and our success can all very well go away tomorrow." These managers didn't have the confidence necessary to make the decisions that would sustain profitable growth.

When a manager has strong self-confidence and poor business results, he perseveres and innovates to find ways to create more value for customers. Even though the short-term looks bleak, he believes the long-term is bright. However, it's not enough just to persevere. Eventually a manager has to actually produce strong business results.

The manager who has strong self-confidence and strong business results is the one who produces true business momentum. She has the confidence to push forward and the resources to invest in future growth.

The practical processes in this book are focused on improving both your tangible organizational results and the intangible, psychological belief you have in your ability to generate even better results in the future.

PREPARE WITH PRECISION TO WIN THE MANAGEMENT 500

For you, Day 1 of a three-year business race is fast approaching. Your goal: to get ready to manage the business or profit center in a way that accelerates positive cash flow in a sustainable manner. What lies in front of you are three years' worth of laps where you will have to be at your very best.

You will have to make difficult decisions on strategy and people, deal with crises, maintain your concentration and the attention of your group members on executing a plan that may change over time, stay focused on your customers, and sustain your effort over the next twelve quarters. Not an easy task.

It's a thirty-six-month race. You can lose the race quickly, but you can't win quickly. You can get so far behind that you'll never make it to the end, but you can't get so far ahead that you can coast in. The first step toward winning the Management 500 is demanding exactness in your preparation for the race.

Larry McReynolds, a highly successful former NASCAR crew chief and author of *How to Become a Winning Crew Chief*, said, "The best way to make sure preparation is complete before you load that car and head to the track is to develop a comprehensive checklist system and adhere to it for everything you do."[15] In Figure 1.2 is a checklist to help you prepare for the business race ahead of you.

FIGURE 1.2 *Pre-Race Checklist*

The Management 500 Pre-Race Checklist

✓ Confidence   ✓ Customer

✓ Enthusiasm   ✓ Organizational Talent

✓ Personal Effectiveness   ✓ Strategic Understanding

✓ Physical   ✓ Priorities

✓ Mental   ✓ Schedule

✓ Industry   ✓ Communication

Confidence Prep

Joe was VP of Operations of a massive business unit, with several billion dollars in total revenue. He was talented in operations and had a good track record. His challenge was he doubted the real value that he brought to the table. He told me, "If I lose this job, I'm done. I'll never be able to regain this status." Consequently, he spent the vast majority of his time trying to either please his boss or figure out what he could do to please his boss.

When the corporation went through a reorganization, and Joe had to interview for the few remaining operational positions, he wasn't able to articulate the value he brought to the organization. One of his subordinates got the position he wanted. It was a devastating blow to an already fragile self-confidence.

Many times a person gets promoted to a key management position because of great performance in an important functional area, such as sales, operations, marketing, or finance. However, if the person's confidence is based on having a certain title, then he or she really has label confidence, not self-confidence. When the person makes a mistake as a manager, his or her self-confidence plummets because it's not based on any internal characteristics.

While you can't always determine your external, tangible business results, you can largely determine your self-confidence. Strengthening self-confidence is a two-step process.

The Process for Strengthening Your Self-Confidence

1. Review your past success stories.

2. Preview your future success stories.

Pounding yourself on the chest and saying, "I am great," will only give you a sore chest. Having someone else tell you you're great is nice, but doesn't strengthen your self-confidence. Those words are the opinion of someone else about you, but not necessarily your opinion about you. The key is to uncover why you succeeded in the past. Here's the first step.

The Process for Reviewing a Past Success Story

Invest five minutes in answering the questions below.

1. What was your goal?

2. What were the obstacles that stood in the way of achieving that goal?

3. How did you persevere?

4. What did it feel like when you achieved the goal?

5. What lessons did you learn from that experience that you can use in your current work situation?

A success is any time you achieved something really meaningful to you. Pause and think back over your lifetime. When was a time you set an important goal, persevered through obstacles, and sustained your performance all the way to success? What was the feeling like, and what lessons did you learn from that experience?

I encourage you to take out three sheets of paper. Take the first, recall one of your past successes, and write down your answers to the five questions above. Then go to the second sheet, think of a success story from a different period in your life, and write down your answers. Then do it one more time, from yet another period—or aspect—of your life. You can do this entire exercise in less than fifteen minutes.

These stories are very valuable because you now have something real that you can go back to in your mind to remind yourself that you have overcome challenges in the past and you can do it again in the future.

The second step to strengthening self-confidence is to preview a future success story.

The Process for Previewing a Future Success Story

Invest five minutes in answering these questions.

1. What do you want to achieve?

2. Why do you want to achieve it?

3. Why do you expect to achieve it?

Hope is not a strategy for success, and neither is hard work. A person can work incredibly hard and hope very sincerely for success, and yet never attain real success. Of the three questions above the most important one is the last one.

Take the three sheets of paper from before and turn them over. Decide on one business outcome you want to achieve and write it down on the first piece of paper. Be as clear as you can about what you specifically want to achieve.

Then write down all the reasons why you want to achieve that desired outcome. What would be the benefits of achieving it to you, your employees, your organization, your customers, and your suppliers?

Then write down why you expect to achieve it. What experience or knowledge or skills or relationships have you and your team developed that causes you to expect to achieve the desired outcome?

Take the next sheet and answer the three questions for another high-priority desired business outcome. Then repeat the process one more time.

Down the road you will need to map out how you will go about achieving each of the desired outcomes and then move into action, but be sure to first take the time to strengthen your self-confidence.

Enhance your belief that you will succeed in the upcoming situation. This is how you drive fast slowly.

Enthusiasm Prep

As a manager, know that other people watch your actions and your body language. If you're just going through the motions to get to the end of the day, everybody will know it even if you say all of the right things.

An intriguing quote I've heard over the years is, "To be enthusiastic, act enthusiastic." That is one I've learned to disagree with. I think if you act enthusiastic when you're not, other people will think you're a fake and they will doubt your sincerity. True enthusiasm comes from a sense of purpose.

The Process for Maintaining Daily Enthusiasm

1. Clarify your purpose for doing what you do.

2. Focus every day on fulfilling your purpose.

What is your purpose as a manager? Why do you do what you do? I call this "PBTP," purpose beyond the paycheck. This one might take several days to think about or even several weeks. If you want to achieve greatness as a manager and win the Management 500, you will have to maintain genuine enthusiasm on a regular basis over an extended period of time. That requires knowing your purpose for doing what you do and focusing on fulfilling that purpose every day.

I've been asked many times over the last twenty-five years how I maintain my enthusiasm so consistently. The answer is really very simple. I have had a very clear purpose and I've stuck to it ever since my college days. Over the years I've been a college coach, a high school teacher, an organizational consultant, an executive coach, a keynote speaker, a workshop facilitator, and an author. However, the common thread through all of these activities has been my purpose—

wanting to work with other people so they achieve great performances. This purpose is what has fueled me all these years.

In his autobiography, Enzo Ferrari said, "Fate is to a good extent
in our own hands if we only know clearly what we want and are stead-
fast in our purpose. A single-mindedness of purpose in pursuing one's
ambition is a force that can overcome many obstacles."[16] From his
purpose of making extraordinary racecars, Ferrari's legacy flowed out,
and it lives on to today. What is your purpose as a manager? Why do
you do what you do?

Personal Effectiveness Prep

The greatest value you bring to your company is the combination of
your values, strengths, and passions. Your company has high priority
outcomes it wants to achieve, and your customers have high priority
outcomes they want to achieve as a result of buying from your
company.

Now here comes the hard part if you want to optimize your effectiveness as a manager. The truly effective manager intentionally intersects his or her strengths and passions with the desired outcomes on a
daily basis, and does it while sticking to his or her values.

When you spend the vast majority of your time deploying your
strengths and passions toward improving important outcomes while
staying within your own values, you begin to clearly see the role you
play in moving business results forward. As you do so, you gain a
greater and greater belief in your ability to succeed in future
situations.

You might be thinking, "Dan, don't managers already do this
every day? Don't they use their strengths and passions to drive better
results for their organizations and for their customers?"

If you asked me that, I would say, "Theoretically, yes, but in reality many times distractions occur. Meetings run over, employees have
personal crises, customers are upset, and suddenly the day is over and
the manager has not used his or her strengths and passions at all. The
key is to *intentionally* intersect these three entities. It just won't happen
without a conscious effort on the part of the manager."

After you write your answers out to the seven questions on page 20,

The Process for Intentionally Intersecting Your Values, Strengths, and Passions with the Desired Outcomes

Invest two minutes in answering each of the following seven questions. Then go back and invest another ten minutes looking over your answers and filling in any missing thoughts.

Internal Assets

1. What are your values? (Values are beliefs that drive behaviors.)

2. What are your strengths? (Strengths are what you do well.)

3. What are your passions? (Passions are what gets you excited.)

External Understanding

4. What are the two most important business outcomes your organization wants to improve this year?

5. What are the two most important outcomes that your customers want to improve this year as a result of working with your organization?

Intentional Intersecting

6. How can you use your strengths and passions in a practical way that will increase the chances of your organization achieving its goals while still operating within your own values?

7. How can you use your strengths and passions in a practical way that will increase the chances of your customers achieving their goals while still operating within your own values?

I encourage you to take out a three-by-five index card and write down a few themes that summarize your values, strengths, and passions.

At the beginning of each work day, take out the card and ask yourself, "How will I use my strengths and passions to drive better results for my organization and/or our customers today?" At the end of each work day, read over your card and ask yourself, "How did I use my strengths and passions today to drive better results for my organization and/or our customers?" In doing so, you will be intentionally intersecting your values, strengths, and passions with the desired outcomes. That's how you remain effective every day.

Physical Prep

Back in the day, experts said that the Internet would replace paper and web conferencing would dramatically reduce travel. Nice try. The last eight planes I flew on were completely sold out. It didn't matter the time of the day or the day or the week or the part of the country I was flying to. Every seat on every plane was filled. So much for no more traveling.

If you want to guide your team to sustainable, profitable growth, you need to bring your best energy to work every day. I'm not encouraging you to work 70 hours a week, but I am urging you to bring your best energy to every hour that you do work. You need to be in good physical shape to guide the myriad details you will encounter. It's not about vanity. It's about having the energy to make steady progress toward improving results.

A big part of Michael Schumacher's success was the extraordinary conditioning he maintained throughout his driving career. Fellow driver Julian Bailey said, "We'd do the qualifying and then he'd go off and play tennis for four or five hours, keep on until late at night for his fitness. He was the fittest then, and in Formula 1 he's the fittest now."[17]

When you're out of shape, you can fight your way through the challenges for maybe five months. You can survive on caffeine and candy to keep you going. And then, boom, you'll hit a wall, and you'll wonder if all this hard work is really worth it. The key is staying fresh and having the energy necessary to take on challenges and opportunities in a way that energizes rather than drains you.

My brother-in-law, Richard Taylor, has a great diet book concept called "The Four-Word Physical Fitness Plan." It will only have two chapters and four words in the whole book.

Chapter One: Eat right.

Chapter Two: Exercise regularly.

It doesn't get much simpler than that. All of the wisdom on physical health can be reduced to those four words: eat right, exercise regularly. What is really crazy is that you and I already know that. The stumbling block is execution. Select your own plan. You know the basic drill: fruits and vegetables are better for you than fries and burgers, three martinis a day really will send you to the doctor, and water is better for you than soda. Jog, lift weights, play basketball or tennis or soccer or racquetball, and get out and move.

The most successful managers I've met stay in shape, pure and simple. They work out early or late or at noon time. They find ways to get it done. Many of them don't like to exercise. They hate to run, but they know the benefits. They would rather have the onion rings, but they want their best energy for the biggest moments. If you want to drive the winning car over the long term, you need to be in great shape.

It's time to get real. What two things are you going to do, or stop doing, to increase your energy and stamina? You don't have to become a world-class athlete, but if you want to accelerate your current business results in a sustainable way, then you may very well need better energy and stamina than you have right now. Don't make a list of twelve things. That's unrealistic. Just select two. Is there some activity you're going to start doing or stop doing? Is there something you're going to start eating or drinking, or stop eating or drinking? Make your decisions and move into action.

Mental Prep

Can you imagine getting into the driver's seat at the Indianapolis 500 never having studied the art and science of racecar driving? Or imagine one day someone taps you on the shoulder and says, "In an hour you're driving in the Daytona 500. I know you've never been in a race before, but you're going to do great." It doesn't work that way.

The best racecar drivers study the details of driving fast in a crowded field. They discuss the experience with other drivers who have gone before them. Many of them have read about what the best drivers in history have accomplished and how they did it. To gain a sense of the degree to which world-class drivers study their sport, I encourage you to read about drivers like Richard Petty, Michael Schumacher, Dale Earnhardt Sr., Jeff Gordon, and Mario Andretti.

To ramp up your success for the next three years, become a student of the art and science of management. As you go through this book, I will recommend a variety of excellent management books. Ask people you respect for the books they've read. Read *BusinessWeek* and *Fortune* magazine regularly. Scan *The Wall Street Journal* every day. Join professional groups to exchange ideas and learn from other executives and managers. If you work as a CEO or key executive in a mid-size business, join useful organizations like Vistage International, which holds seminars for CEOs and key executives. Constantly strengthen your mental preparation.

Leaders are readers. I've always bought into that statement. Be a student of the game of management. Don't be a theorist, be a pragmatist. Jump in and apply the ideas you've learned. Over time you will hone your own philosophy and style of management.

Don't just read and read and read. Read, capture, and apply. Regularly step back from the activity of work and study the intangibles that make for great managers. After you read a chapter in a book or a magazine, ask yourself, "What did I learn that might be useful in moving results forward in my current project, and how will I use this idea?" Then consciously apply the idea as soon as possible. After you apply it, you can make adjustments and improve the application the next time. Constantly prepare yourself for greater success in the future.

What two things are you going to do to better your understanding of management? Is there a specific book you want to read, a course you want to take, a mentor within your company that you want to approach, or a project team that you want to be a part of? If you continue to go forward with your current understanding of management, then you will continue to be the same manager you are today. That isn't going to improve results over the long term.

Industry Prep

If someone asked you to describe the state of the industry you're in, what would you say? What would you base your answers on? Do you have a firm grip on what is happening in your industry right now? What can you do to increase your understanding of your industry? Can you attend your industry's national conferences, join the board of the local or national association for your industry, read pertinent material about your industry, or something else? A variety of activities will help increase your understanding of the industry.

> **The Process for Understanding Your Industry**
>
> Answer these two questions.
>
> 1. What major changes are happening in your industry and how could they affect your business positively or negatively?
>
> 2. What changes outside of your industry will have the greatest positive or negative impact on the future of organizations in your industry?

You don't need to be the preeminent world expert on your industry, but you do need to be aware of the forces that could damage your business and the opportunities you can take advantage of to accelerate your desired business outcomes.

Customer Prep

Understanding industry trends pales in comparison to understanding your customers. Before starting the upcoming race, spend time really understanding your customers. Who are the people that buy the products and services from your business or profit center? What are they like? What trends are affecting them?

The Process for Gaining a Greater Understanding of Your Customers

1. Watch your customers in action. Watch as they purchase and interact with the products and services your organization sells.

2. Talk to your customers in an informal way to find out their perspective on the value they receive from your organization.

3. Spend time as the customer. Purchase a product or a service and see what the experience is like. Try to do so incognito so you can see how you're treated. If you can't be anonymous, have a friend from outside the organization be a customer and discuss what his or her experience was like.

Organizational Talent Prep

What talent do you have in your organization right now to truly accelerate sustainable, profitable growth? By talent, I mean the capacity to add relevant value to customers that they will want and be willing to pay for. What values, strengths, and passions do your employees have that can be deployed to move results forward in a sustainable manner? Focus on understanding the talent in your organization, and don't make decisions about hiring or firing anyone yet.

Invest as much time as you can early on in getting to know the people in your organization. Search for their values, strengths, and passions. Ask your employees what they believe those to be, but also observe them. Soon you will have a clear idea of what different people bring to the table.

It's unlikely you're going to be able to replace everyone so rather than looking at what people do poorly, find out what they have that you can build a winner on. Find out what they do well, what healthy beliefs they consistently demonstrate, and what they have passion for doing.

Talent is the capacity to add value to customers. What talent do you have in your organization that you can build on?

Strategic Understanding Prep

Don't start the race by changing your organization's strategy on Day 1. You simply don't know enough to make a sweeping strategic change. Even if you've been in charge of the organization for six years, don't start the next three years by introducing a new strategic direction that you came up with on your own. You still need to gather input and gain support for it to succeed. Otherwise you'll end up with "my strategy," not "our strategy," to win. Unless you plan on doing every single activity in your organization all by yourself, I encourage you to slow down and work toward the development of a new strategy with the other key members of your team.

The most important first step in developing a better strategy is to understand the current strategy. A strategy describes an organization and guides future decisions regarding the organization. Below are seven questions to help you describe the current strategy of your organization or profit center. Don't be intimidated by the number of questions. All you need are a few sentences to answer each question.

If the truth is that there is no clear answer to a question, then write that down. For example, if your organization has fifteen different purposes that employees think it is trying to fulfill, then just write down, "The answer is unclear."

Answer these seven questions in order to help clarify the current strategy for your organization. Twenty minutes may seem like very little time, but if your organization's strategy is clear, you will be able to write your answers down quickly. If it is not clear, then that will become very obvious as you struggle to answer these questions.

Until you really understand your organization's current strategy, you won't be able to effectively reinforce it or redesign it. If you find that the current strategy is unclear and constantly changing, that's

The Process for Understanding Your Current Strategy

Invest twenty minutes in answering these questions.

1. What are the most important business outcomes you want to achieve in terms of revenues, costs, and profits over the next three years?

2. What is the purpose of your organization?

3. What is primarily driving decisions in your organization? Is it to offer the best product/service, to serve the needs of a specific market, to provide the best customized solution, to offer the lowest price, or to leverage a learned body of knowledge?

4. How would your customers describe the products and services they buy from your organization?

5. How would your customers describe their relationship with your organization?

6. What value do your customers think they currently receive when they buy from your organization and how does your organization deliver that value?

7. What are the behaviors your employees currently demonstrate on a consistent basis?

OK. Go ahead and write it down. You want to know what you're working from in order to improve it in the future.

Priorities Prep

You're not going to change or accomplish twenty things successfully in the next six months. Please trust me on that. Whether you're working with a group you've been in charge of for many years or a brand new group, trying to accomplish too much too fast is a recipe for disaster. Many times I've seen managers be unrealistic and go after far too many objectives and activities simultaneously. In the end, they achieved very little in terms of improving important results.

Why not reverse the challenge? Instead of saying, "I have what it takes to go after twenty goals at once and achieve all of them," just say, "I have the courage to select the two most important outcomes to improve over the next six months, and we're going to focus on improving those two." You can make progress on two important objectives. That's realistic. That's how you generate *sustainable*, profitable growth. Accomplish two important objectives, and then consider moving on to something else if your progress on those two has been really significant.

The Process for Establishing Your Priorities

Invest ten minutes in answering these questions.

1. What two outcomes can you realistically improve in the next six months that would have the greatest positive impact on moving your business forward in a profitable and sustainable manner?

2. What outcomes are you not going to emphasize in the next six months?

Your answers might not please Wall Street analysts or even your boss, but the goal of this book is not to please those people. The goal is to help you win the race for sustainable, profitable growth. By defining the two most important outcomes to improve and the ones you are not going to focus on, you will help your employees enormously toward focusing their efforts. When a manager has twenty important objectives, the employees don't know where to spend their time.

When Mark Hurd took over from Carly Fiorina in 2005 as CEO of Hewlett-Packard, he put on a classic textbook example of how to prepare for a new management position. After studying the HP business, the industry, and his employees, he decided on a few important outcomes to improve and one important outcome not to focus on.[18]

Fiorina had introduced a series of new strategies each year for three years in a row. She reorganized her business units, she bought Compaq, and she continually spoke to the business media about how she was reinventing HP.

Hurd stepped in and largely avoided the media. Many people thought he would reinvent HP once again. He didn't go there. When he did speak to the media, he said there would be no changes to the strategy. He made it clear he was going to focus on simplifying the business and improving execution. He clarified what different departments were responsible for and what they weren't responsible for. He scheduled his time to be with his employees, not with the media. Within those first six months, the business performance improved significantly.

Scheduling Prep

All of this talk about preparation and priority outcomes means nothing until you place activities on your calendar. Where you spend your time speaks volumes about your business priorities.

If you say securing two new major customers is critical to your organization's success over the next six months and you schedule no time with prospects or your sales team in the first month, then you're fooling yourself. If you don't get into this race with a prepared schedule, you will quickly find your time being eaten up by other people's priorities.

Having all the industry and company knowledge in the world does nothing to improve results if you don't select and execute specific activities to improve those results. The key is to carefully select those six activities, put them on your calendar, and make them more important than anything else on your calendar. Don't let the urgency of the moment get in the way of doing the stuff that really matters.

The Process for Scheduling Your Priority Activities

1. Select your top desired outcome for the next six months.

2. Identify the three key activities you will do over the next thirty days that you think will have the greatest positive impact on improving that outcome.

3. Put those activities on your calendar.

4. Select the second most important desired outcome for the next six months.

5. Identify the three key activities you will do over the next thirty days that you think will have the greatest positive impact on improving that outcome.

6. Put those activities on your calendar.

7. Now fill in the rest of your calendar with what other people need from you.

Communication Prep

Before you walk into an important meeting with your employees or a private one-on-one conversation with one of them, clarify the key messages you want the other individual or individuals to focus on. If you begin business relationships by giving jumbled messages, even in your relationships with current employees, it's going to be very hard for you to clear things up later on. Decide on the two or three main points you want to keep everyone focused on, write them down, and practice saying them in a clear and concise manner.

One of my clients successfully focused her communications on the importance of improving basic operations throughout her business unit. She brought this point home in every single communication, and it worked. She was able to keep the attention of the entire profit center that covered one-third of the United States on improving the fundamentals of operations. Customer satisfaction scores started rising—as did top-line sales and bottom-line profits.

The Process of Stating Your Key Messages Clearly

1. Take out a sheet of paper. Write down the key messages you want to get across to your new, or current, team as you prepare them for success over the next three years. Write down every important message you can think of.

2. Identify the one to three most important messages you want to focus on over the next six months.

3. Build those one, two, or three messages into every speech, voicemail, e-mail, and private conversation you give. Stick with these three messages for at least the next six months. Keep the attention of your group focused on the few things that matter the most. Don't introduce any other key messages during that six-month time period.

THE IMPORTANCE OF PREPARATION

The race usually favors the driver who is better prepared. That is particularly true for the longer and more challenging races. Three years to consistently generate sustainable, profitable growth is a long, challenging race. The better prepared you are at the beginning of the race the better your chances for success will be at the end. Keep in mind that preparation is an ongoing affair. You don't prepare to win once, and then not worry about it again. Instead focus every day on being prepared to make that day a successful part of the overall race.

To help with your preparation, I encourage you to read *The Effective Executive* by Peter Drucker very carefully.[19] This is Drucker's shortest and finest book and will help prepare you for the business race that lies ahead. Particularly focus on Chapters 2 and 4, which have powerful insights on leveraging your strengths and knowing where your time is going.

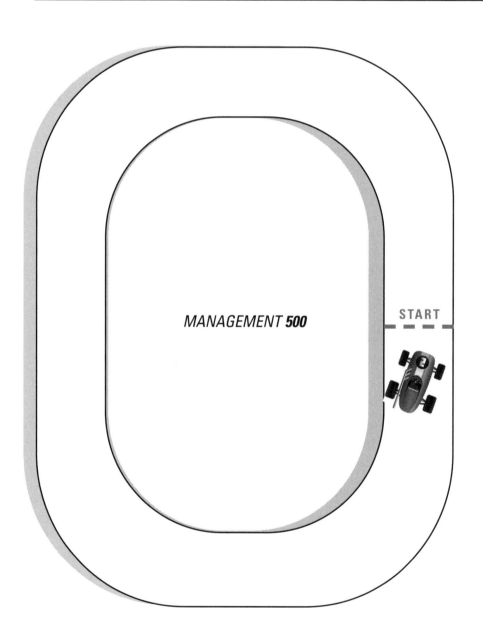

CHAPTER TWO

MANAGEMENT *500*

START

QUALIFY FOR THE
POLE POSITION

> "These days, a good qualifying program is more important than ever because, no matter what series you are racing, it can be very difficult to pass on the track. It only makes sense that when you want to be the first to cross the finish line, starting at the front gives you an advantage."
> —**Larry McReynolds, veteran NASCAR crew chief and NASCAR television broadcaster**[1]

The most important starting position for a racecar driver to be in is the pole position. The driver in the pole position is in the inside front row position at the beginning of the race. The reason the pole position is so important is that the driver in that spot literally starts the race with an advantage over every other driver. Quite simply, the drivers who start in the pole position most often win the most races. That isn't true for every race or every driver, but over the long run it certainly holds true.

How does a driver get the pole position?

It's not awarded using a lottery, rotation, or seniority basis. A driver has to earn the pole position over all the other drivers for each race. Every driver—young, old, experienced, inexperienced, male, or female—has the same opportunity to qualify for the pole position.

The starting positions for the race are determined during the qualifying laps that are driven usually the day before or two days before the actual race begins. The driver with the fastest time during the qualifying stage is awarded the pole position.

The main objective for the driver in the pole position is to gain some early victories. If the driver can maintain the lead going into and coming out of the first pit stop, then he or she has a greater chance of winning the overall race. Being in the pole position doesn't guarantee success, but over the long run consistently starting with an advantage generates the most victories.

THE POLE POSITION IN THE MANAGEMENT 500

You're now thirty days away from starting the three-year race to significantly increase sustainable, profitable growth. You're either taking over a new organization or profit center, or you're beginning a new three-year race with your current group. You have thirty days to get to know the situation, the most important desired business outcomes, and the people in the organization.

Imagine in thirty days starting the race with a great advantage that can lead to some early victories. If you use the next thirty days effectively, you can qualify for the pole position and gain momentum quickly. On the other hand, if you're not careful, you can seriously injure your career and be eliminated from the race altogether. It doesn't matter how successful you've been in the past or how many management races you've won. You still will benefit greatly if you qualify for the pole position in the upcoming race whether your employees, suppliers, and customers already know you or not.

Notice that the pole position goes to the driver who races the fastest lap during the qualifying round. It doesn't go to the most durable driver or the oldest or youngest driver. If you want the pole position as a business manager, you need to demonstrate speed in the next thirty days. Your early victories are going to fall into two categories: relationships and results. By making immediate progress toward strengthening relationships with individuals throughout your organization, you can gain the trust and support necessary to improve organizational performance right away. By finding the low-hanging fruit in terms of results, you can begin to demonstrate success immediately.

The Process for Qualifying for the Pole Position as a Business Manager

1. Announce you're going to take the first thirty days to get to know the people in your organization.

2. Make a list of all the key people who can affect the success of your organization or profit center.

3. Schedule a twenty-minute face-to-face meeting with each individual on the list.

4. Follow up with each person within three days after the meeting.

As a manager, you're in a relationship business. Don't ever forget that. The faster you can build trusting relationships with your employees, suppliers, and customers, the faster you can improve results. Relationships require time, as in face time. For example, let's say you have 150 key people who can affect your organization's results. This includes your employees, suppliers, business partners, key customers, and executive team members. You can adjust those numbers to fit your situation.

At the beginning of these thirty days, communicate to everyone that you are going to invest the next thirty days in getting to know people and the business situation. Make it clear you are not going to attend department meetings or industry meetings or headquarter meetings. You are going to be meeting with people on a one-to-one or small group basis. Make it clear you are not yet available to start solving problems or resolving issues.

If you don't communicate that very clearly up front, then within the first five minutes of the first day, people will start to reach out to you and eat up your time.

Relationships inside Your Organization

Schedule a twenty-minute face-to-face private meeting with each employee. This includes department heads, staff members, and certainly the members of the administrative assistant team. During those twenty minutes, dedicate your total focus to the other person. Meet in a conference room or somewhere comfortable outside of your office. Do *not* bring in a cell phone, laptop computer, Blackberry, or any access to the outside world. Do *not* allow interruptions to occur. This whole meeting is only going to last for twenty minutes. You want the other person to see that he or she has your undivided attention.

Stay very calm and don't take notes while you're meeting with the person. Just make eye contact and listen. This is a conversation, not a job interview for either of you. Use the person's name several times during the conversation. Ask comfortable questions such as, "What's your role here? What do you enjoy about it? What would make it even better for you? What are you proud of during the past six months? What are you good at doing? What are your passions? How do you think we add value to customers? How do you think we could add more value to customers? What questions do you have for me?"

At the end of twenty minutes, say, "Thanks for taking the time for us to get to know each other better." After the conversation is over immediately write the person a handwritten note that you can send to him or her so it is received within three days. Making the note personal and relevant to the individual won't take more than three minutes. Don't write the same thing to each person. Reference something that was actually discussed in the conversation. Let the person know that you're thinking about him or her as an individual and not as just a member of the staff.

Of course, this isn't a "one time and we're done forever" conversation. The purpose of this conversation is simply to build a foundation for future conversations and what will hopefully become a strong, or stronger, relationship.

After you write the note, relax for a few minutes and then meet with the next person. If you have a hundred employees, that will take fifty hours. Spread that over the next thirty days and you're looking at an hour or two each day dedicated to strengthening relationships with individual staff members. Remember, as a manager you're in a relationship business. If you have more than 100 employees, then communicate with the masses via voicemail and e-mail and let everyone know you will be meeting with them in group meetings over the next six months.

Relationships with Suppliers

You never win the Management 500 by yourself or just with your employees. Someone outside of your organization is helping you to create and deliver value to customers. A key outside group is made up of your suppliers. Say you have ten key suppliers. Again, adjust the numbers to your situation. During the thirty-day qualifying stage, go meet with each of these suppliers for ninety minutes in person at his or her office or at a restaurant. If you can't get something worthwhile accomplished in ninety minutes, then you're not going to get it done in four hours either.

Invest the first twenty or thirty minutes in getting to know the individual better as a person. Just relax and have a conversation. Then spend the next hour garnering perspective from the person about the business. Ask what the person has found to be effective and not so effective in working with your organization. Don't try to defend or trash any of your employees. Just listen. Take notes if it helps.

When you recap the conversation in writing, mention things that came up in both parts of the meeting. Thank the person for his or her time. Keep a copy of the letter or e-mail so you can quickly refer to it the next time the two of you meet.

Relationships with Other Key Partners

Some businesses have other key partners such as franchisees, dealer principals, key distributors, and so on. During these thirty days, meet with each of these key partners. For the sake of this example, say you have twenty key partners. Follow the same pattern: relaxed conversations combined with seeking out their opinions on business issues. Follow up every meeting with a letter or e-mail. I suggest handwritten or typed letters that have some handwriting on them. E-mail makes for a lousy first written communication. There's too much at stake in all of these relationships to not get off to the best possible start.

Relationships with Customers

Make a list of the ten most important customers you have, even if it means including someone who represents a larger group of like-minded customers. Again, ninety minutes is long enough. You want to establish and/or strengthen a foundation with that person based on listening for understanding and following up so he or she knows you really heard what was said. You're not going to resolve customer issues at this first meeting. You're working for understanding, not resolution.

Relationships with Your Executive Team

And now the folks who are going to work with you the most intimately over the next three years: your executive team. Let's say there are ten members on your executive team. After your initial meeting with each of them, set up another one-hour one-on-one meeting to discuss the four business questions on the next page. Give each person the questions a week or so ahead of your meeting so they can come prepared to discuss their answers. The answers to these four questions can help lead you to the fastest way to achieve some positive business results. Those results can help build momentum for bigger results in the future.

After you've discussed these questions individually with each member of the executive team, set up two two-hour meetings for the whole executive team to come together. At these meetings, discuss the four questions again, and also share the insights you've gained from your suppliers, customers, key business partners, and employees. As a group, discuss what two or three items can be focused on immediately to gain some traction in terms of achieving some early victories, both

The Process for Finding Low-Hanging Revenue Growth and Productivity Enhancement Opportunities

1. What products or services do you currently sell that customers will buy more of if you increased the quality of them significantly?

2. What products or services do you currently sell that some of your current customers have not yet bought but will benefit from and how can you communicate the value to those customers?

3. What products or services do you currently sell that potential customers will benefit from and who are those potential customers?

4. How can you deliver the same value to customers that you're currently working with in a more efficient and productive way?

in terms of specific business results and in terms of stronger relationships with employees, suppliers, key partners, and/or customers.

Keep in mind that intangibles drive tangible results. If you're doing the math, here's what your time allotment could look like for 150 people in the next thirty days:

Fifty hours—100 current employees

Fifteen hours—ten suppliers

Thirty hours—twenty key partners

Fifteen hours—ten customers

Fourteen hours—ten executive team members, in individual and group meetings

That's 124 hours in thirty days or thirty-one hours a week for a solid month. If you do that, you can make progress on a variety of intangibles: trust, understanding, awareness, and esprit de corps. Of course, this is just a starting point, but that's the whole point. You just want to qualify to start the race in the best possible position that you can.

Thirty-one hours a week for four straight weeks in building relationships and gaining understanding means that you will have to say no to a variety of other possibilities. However, my goal is for you to win the Management 500, and that's exactly why I want you to focus on relationships for the first thirty days. The more you increase your chances for success at the beginning of the race, the better your chances will be at the end of it.

WAYS TO LOSE THE POLE POSITION

Sustaining your focus for thirty days is a lot of work. The pole position is not just given to a racecar driver easily. The person has to earn it. As a manager, you have to work hard to be prepared to step into the qualifying stage and handle it well. Plus you can lose any advantage you've built up very easily before the race starts. You won't necessarily get fired for losing the pole position, but if you lose it you will have just made it that much harder to win the Management 500 over the next three years. Here are a number of ways to lose the pole position.

Tell an off-color joke. In an attempt to be seen as "just one of the gang," you may be tempted to tell an off-color joke to loosen other people up. I encourage you to put that idea on the shelf. You're the boss. You don't have to be a dictator, but you also don't have to operate with a locker room mentality.

Dress inappropriately. Wearing a $2,000 suit for a twenty-minute conversation is overkill. In all likelihood, wearing a pair of jeans with sandals and a t-shirt isn't hitting the mark either. Here's a suggestion: think one notch better. Whatever your employees wear, dress one notch better. Of course, if you think they dress like slobs and you want to get the point across that you want to improve the dress code, then dress two or three notches better.

Gossip about an employee. If you learn something about one of your employees, you will turn yourself into a very weak executive if you spread gossip about the person, even if it's true. You have to hold yourself to a higher standard as the boss.

Make insulting comments. Insulting an employee in a group setting during your first thirty days—or ever, for that matter—is going to damage relationships for a very long time, especially if you make the insult personal and subjective. If you say your vice-president of finance is just an accountant and can't see the big picture, then everyone is going to wonder what negative things you say about them.

Make assumptions. Don't assume you know someone just because of the person's role, race, gender, height, or weight. If you say an overweight employee can't be effective in a face-to-face customer relations position because customers won't respect the person, then the rest of the employees will wonder what assumption you've made about them.

Don't pay attention. If you really want to turn a person off, nod your head while he or she is talking, and then in your subsequent comments make it clear you weren't listening to a word that was said.

Make inappropriate comments. Say to an employee that you think another employee is fat, sexy, hot, or boring. Or insult a long-term supplier or customer in front of a dozen of your employees. These are ways to lose any advantage that you might have had in terms of strong relationships at the start of the race.

Be sarcastic. Dripping sarcasm can be an instant relationship killer. Stay on the alert to treat people with respect. Trust me when I say they are watching your actions while they are listening to your words.

Be two-faced. If you want to really turn people off, be very positive with them when they share their ideas with you, and then make fun of their ideas when you talk to other people. Eventually this will play itself out and people will find out that you were extremely insincere with them.

WAYS TO CRASH AND BE ELIMINATED FROM THE RACE

The best way I know of for a manager to crash and be knocked out of the Management 500 is to lie during those first thirty days. When you get caught lying in the first month, people have no choice but to ask you to leave. The thought process is, "If this person is going to lie this early, how bad will it get later on? How will I ever know when I can trust this person?'

One well-known example of crashing and being eliminated happened in December 2001. A person had just been hired as the head football coach to resurrect the University of Notre Dame football team. Five days later it was discovered that twenty years earlier he had lied on his resume and had never changed it. On the resume, the person stated he had earned a master's degree from NYU–Stony Brook, a school that never existed. He had taken two courses at NYU, but never graduated. He also said he had earned three letters in football at the University of New Hampshire. The problem was the school said he had not even played in one game.

Notre Dame initially supported the person when the discrepancies became known because he promised the school that there were no other hidden secrets. When Notre Dame discovered he had lied about other things as well, the school asked for his resignation.

Can you imagine the embarrassment this created both for the individual and the organization? Beyond that, can you imagine preparing for your whole career to take over an exciting position, and then to have the race ended before it ever started just because you told a lie and never cleared it up with the truth? You may not win every business race you enter, but be on the alert to avoid the critical damage you can do to your career through something as devastating as lying on your resume.

FINAL THOUGHTS

Ok, that's it. You have thirty days to qualify for the pole position. You want to optimize your relationships and your understanding of the key results you need to impact right away to get the collective group headed toward significant, sustainable, and profitable growth.

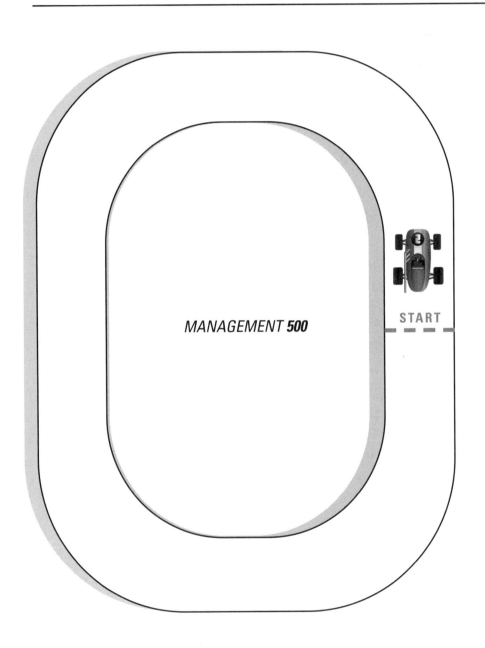

CHAPTER THREE

MANAGEMENT 500

START

START YOUR *ENGINE*

"Ladies and gentlemen, start your engines."

The difference is dramatic.

Fifteen minutes before a race starts and fifteen minutes after a race starts represents the difference between complete calmness and utter chaos. After being introduced to the crowd, a racecar driver calmly gets into the car, locks the steering wheel into place, straps the five-point seat belt on, checks the gauges and switches, and hits the battery switch to get the electrical systems up and running.

Then the most famous introduction in all of sports is announced: "Ladies and gentlemen, start your engines." The driver then hits the start switch, warms the engine, and follows the pace car onto the track. Every car in the race is in the position that was earned during the qualifying laps. During the warm-up laps the drivers weave from side to side to scrub their tires to keep old rubber from sticking to the tires and to evenly warm their tires.

Then the pace car exits, the green flag waves or the red lights go off, and the actual race begins. Suddenly the preparation is over, the qualifying is complete, and the drivers are accelerating to between 160 and 230 mph. For roughly the next three hours 100 percent concentration is required on the part of the driver and his or her team to win the race. The way a driver begins a race will often determine how he or she ends it. If it's a 500-mile race, the first fifty miles are very important. The driver needs to stay in contention by deciding when to take chances and when to play it safe.

THE START OF THE MANAGEMENT 500

When you've completed your thirty days of getting to know your business situation, you are now officially beginning your three-year march toward generating significant, sustainable, and profitable growth. Just like a racecar driver going through the warm-up laps, you have one day at the most to get acclimated before your professional life is going 200 mph.

Then you have calls and e-mails from employees, customers, suppliers, board members, peers, and higher ranking executives all wanting a piece of your time. You now are expected to attend meetings that seem to have no end and no limit. You are expected to make progress immediately toward key business outcomes as well as resolve long-standing issues with a variety of people. The race has begun and there's no turning back. It is now your responsibility to know when to push the car faster and when to take a break.

So what should you not do when the race begins? Three years is twelve quarters. How you perform during the first quarter will largely determine how you finish the race three years later. There are two things I recommend that you *not* do during the first three months of the Management 500:

• Don't fire large groups of people in order to reduce costs.

• Don't announce a new strategic plan for your organization.

I know you're excited to demonstrate great results. You may feel in your gut that your organization has too many employees and that you could produce as much value for customers with a lot fewer. You may want to show your boss and your shareholders that you can improve the bottom line by reducing costs and that you have the guts to make the tough calls. Don't do it. Don't fire anybody in order to reduce costs. Remember, it's a three-year race. If you tick people off and/or frighten them by firing their colleagues during your first quarter, you will undermine your chances for success later on. You have a lot of other things to focus on, and you don't need to end the race just as it's starting.

Second, don't walk into your first management meeting and announce the new strategic direction for the organization. Even if you've thought it through and are confident that you are on the right track, no pun intended, don't announce it. Keep your future strategic thoughts to yourself, and work instead on gaining some momentum both with results and with people before you change the direction of the organization.

SEVEN KEY AREAS AT THE BEGINNING OF THE BUSINESS RACE

In time, you will work on things like clarifying the mission, vision, and values of your organization. You will collaborate with other people to establish the strategic framework for making decisions, the organizational chart to support that strategy, and the planned activities that will need to be executed successfully to win the race. You will develop a communications platform and help employees see how critically important they are to the success of the organization. In reality, your employees expect you to deliver on those big-picture items—but not in the first ninety days. You have other issues that have to be addressed first.

In coaching dozens of executives during the time they started a new three-year race, I have found the following seven items to be the most critical during the first quarter of the first year:

- Customer concerns

- Key partner promises

- Revenue growth

- Cost reduction

- Employee relationships

- Disastrous employees

- Personal habits

Customer Concerns

Sometimes revenue growth comes from customers simply being happier with your organization. During the thirty-day qualifying period you reached out to customers to find out what was on their minds and you observed them in action. Did you pick up anything that could be resolved very quickly?

What did you learn about the customers from your employees? Intensify your search for customer concerns by asking your employees what they've heard from customers. Is there anything they are hearing from customers that could be resolved right away? How about your suppliers? Perhaps they've come across some inside information about what is frustrating your customers. Maybe phone calls aren't being returned or directions are misleading or commitments are not being kept.

Once you land on three common customer complaints, work to immediately resolve those issues in ways that customers will spread the word about what a great job your organization has done.

One example is a customer hotline. Many times customers get frustrated because they go through a seemingly endless number of electronic messages and prompts in order to get their issues resolved. Can you create a customer hotline for the next ninety days where an actual person answers the phone and provides an answer or works to get the answer and then personally calls the customer back?

At the end of the ninety days, you can evaluate whether or not it was a good investment. In the meantime, keep the communication with your customers very active. Let them know that the hotline is available, and then every thirty days give them a progress report on the hotline. You may find that the same two complaints are being reiterated over and over again. After solving those two problems, you can then let customers know that you appreciate their insights and that those issues have been resolved. If no new issues pop up, then you can communicate that the hotline has been shut down.

You can extend the hotline concept by placing an employee on site with your best customers. That way they have someone to turn to immediately with concerns. Of course, that may be too exorbitant or impractical for your business, but the concept can be applied in a variety of ways: daily phone calls, a weekly visit, a ninety-minute e-mail response policy, and so on.

One effective mechanism may be for you to set up a Customer Council during your first ninety days. Bring together a panel of four to six customers each month and just ask them open-ended questions about the value they receive from your organization, what they like about the products and services, what they don't like, and what would make the transfer of value better for them. Keep the discussion to an hour and a quarter, provide a meal, and get them back to their day jobs.

The keys are to demonstrate that you and your employees listen to your customers, consider what has been said, and take action quickly on resolving, or attempting to resolve, key customer issues. Then don't brag about what you've done. Just do it, and let the customers brag to other customers and prospective customers about all of the good things that are happening at your organization.

Key Partner Promises

If you have franchisees or dealer principals or some other type of key business partners, it is very important to begin the race together on solid footing. One way I've seen managers get knocked off the track is by not working to understand what promises have been made to these key business partners in the past. The franchisee or dealer principal is working off of one understanding and the manager is operating off of a different one.

During the first ninety days go to each key business partner and ask for his or her understanding of the business relationship. You might hear that someone was promised a new location or a new set of financials. If this promise is in writing and has been cosigned by someone still in your organization, then determine if you can fulfill that promise. If it can't be realistically fulfilled, then search for other ways to add value to that key business partner.

If the business promise was not written down, then interact with your business partner on a good faith basis. Take the person at their word, and see if you can fulfill that promise. If you can't, then see what you can do to improve their situation. Clearly demonstrate that you are not trying to take advantage of anyone, but that you also have to keep the consideration of the overall business in mind.

This is a very sensitive topic. There's a very good chance that these key business partners have been around for a very long time, and that they have worked with several managers who preceded you. They can become extremely frustrated with broken promises, lose faith in the organization, and look for other organizations to join. It's your job to strengthen those relationships, and you're not going to do that by avoiding the topic of past promises made.

Be proactive, find out the other person's understanding, put all the cards on the table, and then communicate with complete honesty. Everyone knows that situations change, but that doesn't make it any less frustrating when it happens again. You can't generate sustainable, profitable growth without these franchisees, dealer principals, or distributors.

You need a strong relationship based on honesty and a commitment to do what is right both ways. It doesn't mean you have to keep a ridiculous commitment that was made in the past, but it also doesn't mean that you can leave your partners stranded. They may have invested a lot of their own money based on a past agreement. It does you no good to leave them hanging out to dry.

Revenue Growth

Looking for cost savings is important, and I'll talk about that in a few minutes, but you can't save your way to three years of sustainable, profitable growth. You also have to grow revenues. In the first ninety days, you're not going to create an innovative product or service. You're going to have to grow revenues with the products and services you have right now. The key is redeploying what you have at your disposal.

> **The Process for Increasing Short-Term Revenues Using Your Existing Products and Services**
>
> 1. Emphasize specific promotions.
>
> 2. Reposition a product or service.
>
> 3. Leverage hot trends in the marketplace.
>
> 4. Adjust the price of a specific product or service.

Here are four ways to redeploy your current products and services to generate short-term revenue growth: promotions, repositioning, leveraging hot trends, and pricing.

Select one item in your current product/service mix and promote it to increase sales. If you sell lawn mowers in retail stores, select one lawn mower and put it out in front of all of the others. Give it a special display. Have someone stand by the lawn mower, demonstrate its specific features, and answer questions from customers. Sometimes just by highlighting a product, you will increase sales of that product. Notice what happens when the Walt Disney Company pulls out one of their old films from their vault, sells it as a video or DVD, and promotes it heavily. Many times sales of that old movie jump through the roof.

Take a product that has been associated with one age group for a long time and reposition it for a different age group. Could you take one of your current offerings and position it differently to increase sales? If you run an ice cream store known for great products, can you reposition it as a destination for family bonding? If you run a school supplies business, can you reposition it as a one-stop solution for academic needs with connections to private tutors and on-line courses?

Look outside your business. What are the latest trends in society? Is there anything in your current product/service mix that could be combined with a hot trend to speed up your short-term revenues? Is there some story that's getting a lot of airtime on the news that you could respond to in an innovative way? When the Harry Potter books were all the rage, many local bookstores created story times where kids of all ages could gather to discuss their favorite Harry Potter stories.

Lowering prices, or raising them, can move sales quickly, but be careful with this one. Customers may feel they are getting a great deal or that they are moving up on the socioeconomic ladder when they react to a new price point, but dramatically moving prices can come back to haunt a business or an industry. The housing boom and bust is an example of how new pricing can move products quickly, and come back to hurt future sales. It doesn't do much good to increase short-term sales only to ruin your brand's reputation. A good filter to keep in mind is this: "Does this pricing move help to support what we want to be known for in the marketplace?" If it doesn't, be wary.

Cost Reduction

The other side of the profitability coin is reducing costs. For now, do not consider firing employees to reduce costs. Instead challenge yourself and your employees, key partners, and suppliers to find ways to reduce operating costs. Keep in mind that a savings in time, activities, effort, and carrying costs can all lead to cost reductions.

Consider each question on the next page, write down your answers, and then move on to the next question. Get a variety of people involved in answering the questions. Find representatives from each of the different departments who have varying lengths of stay at your organization. Sometimes the most veteran person will see where complexity and cost have crept into the organization, and other times a relatively new person will have an insight that no one else can see.

The best racecar drivers and their crews study every aspect of their cars and the different tracks they run on to find ways to improve performance. Jeff Gordon wrote, "On Tuesday morning the over-the-wall crew and the entire road crew meet with the crew chief to go

The Process for Reducing Costs in the First Ninety Days

Invest sixty minutes to answer these questions.

1. Are there any redundancies in terms of activities throughout your organization?

2. Are you creating add-ons to your products or services that are not adding any additional value to your customers?

3. Are there ways to complete a project in less time without reducing the value to your customers?

4. Are there ways to reduce inventory without reducing your delivery time to customers?

5. Are there times when your organization is buying in bulk to save money per item only to find itself throwing away excess items?

over track notes from the previous race. Tire specialists, engineers, the gasman, the jackman, and all the mechanics go through every detail of the race. Did the tires wear the way we expected? Did the temperatures in the car stay where we thought they would? How did our lap times improve or get worse as we made various adjustments?"[1]

It's important for you to do the same thing. Make it clear to your employees, key business partners, and suppliers that constantly searching for ways to reduce costs is a critical habit to start early and maintain over the long term.

After you have assembled the list of answers for each question, begin to make decisions as to what you and the other members of the organization are going to actually do to start reducing costs. Don't try to do everything on your lists. Just select three things you are going to do immediately. Keep track of the results and communicate those results to everyone. When you've made reasonable progress on the first three items, move to the next three. Steadily work to remove costs in every area, and, of course, keep doing this over the next three years.

Employee Relations

The first ninety days that you're actually in the race sets the standard for how you will behave over the next three years, and this is never truer than in terms of the relationships you build with your employees. If you stop conversing with employees after the thirty-day qualifying period, they will know that you were just putting on a show.

Always keep in mind that it is your employees in combination with your key business partners and suppliers who deliver value to customers. It's partly you, and mostly them. You're the manager for a reason. The job of the manager is to guide the available resources to improve business results in a sustainable way, and human resources are still the most valuable resources.

Of course, you can't spend all of your time building relationships with employees. This isn't a counseling center that you're running. Part of the art of management is finding the right balance between building relationships with employees, suppliers, and key business partners and focusing on revenue growth and cost containment opportunities. I can't tell you what the right balance should be for you, but I do know that at the end of every month you need to make progress in all of those areas.

Look for a combination of individual meetings, small group gatherings, and consistent communication from you to the overall team via handwritten notes, e-mail, voicemail, webcasts, and podcasts. If none of your employees have heard from you in any format for an entire month, then that's a big problem.

One critically important subset of your overall organization is your executive team, which is made up of the individuals whom you will work with to make key decisions and implement planned activities. I've seen executives spend so much time with their employees and suppliers that they leave the members of the executive team wondering whether or not they matter. Those folks matter a lot. Provide them with more one-on-one time than anyone else during those first ninety days.

Disastrous Employees

A disastrous employee is one who delivers poor-to-mediocre results while continuously acting like a jerk and ticking people off. Is that specific enough, or should I go into more detail?

During your first ninety days you are likely to run into The Disastrous Employee Syndrome, which is what happens when managers choose to ignore the disastrous employee. In some cases, you will be the person who has chosen to ignore this walking time bomb of an employee. In other cases, you will inherit a disastrous employee when you take over a business or profit center.

Either way, it's up to you to face reality and make a decision. If you're aware of a disastrous employee, and even more importantly if other employees know that you're aware of a disastrous employee, and you choose to do nothing, then the problem is no longer about your employee's behavior. The problem now is with your lack of courage to intervene and do something, which is not exactly what your best employees are looking for in their manager.

This is akin to a racecar crew chief knowing that a certain mechanic is a poor performer and has an acid attitude, but not being willing to confront the person. Eventually that mechanic is going to hurt the whole team's chance of winning the race. Even more important, the other members of the racecar team will know that the crew chief allows disastrous employees to be part of the team. This may very well cause several of the members to join another racing team.

Why do managers allow disastrous employees to stay on board?

The short answer is rationalization. Managers I've worked with have a host of reasons not to deal directly with a disastrous employee in the first ninety days. Here are some of the rationalizations I've heard (with my responses in parentheses):

"I really don't want to start things on a negative note. I want to create a positive environment." (A superficially positive environment where you act as though things are wonderful even when they're obviously not is not a good start. Behind your back employees will say, "Either he's blind, stupid, or gutless if he really thinks things are going well everywhere.")

"That employee isn't really that bad." (You're trying to win an extremely challenging race: three consecutive years of significant, sustainable, and profitable growth. Do you think you're going to win with employees who "really aren't that bad"?)

"I don't have time right now to deal with this person." (How much of your time and energy are you giving up listening to employees, suppliers, and customers complain about this disastrous employee?)

"I haven't really seen the person do anything too awful." (Well then get your antennae up and start watching. It's possible that eight of your employees just want the person fired, but it's also possible the person really is an incompetent jerk. Don't let your personal feelings for the person gloss over reality.)

"I don't have to deal directly with this person so it's not really that big a deal." (Yes, you're right. However, a lot of other people have to deal with him and they think his lack of communication, constantly being late and unprepared, and rude comments are a very big deal.)

Why does getting rid of a disastrous employee increase your chances of winning the Management 500?

If you've ever dealt with a disastrous employee for any length of time, you already know the answer. A disastrous employee eats up your time and energy both in terms of dealing directly with the individual and dealing with all of the people who are irritated by this individual.

Second, having a disastrous employee hurts the overall performance of the group. Everyone has to work that much harder just to overcome the disastrous employee's mistakes and out-and-out failures. Your employees have to work twice as hard just to maintain their performance levels.

Third, and most importantly, you set the standard for all of the managers below you to keep disastrous employees. If you are not willing to confront this person or get rid of him or her, then why should any of your managers confront or get rid of disastrous employees that report to them? Just by simply avoiding a disastrous employee you have automatically weakened the overall performance of your organization. Not exactly the way to start a winning race, is it?

How does a manager remove a disastrous employee?

If you don't get serious with a disastrous employee in the first ninety days, then it's just going to be that much harder in the future. If you've received multiple complaints about an employee, here's what I suggest you do. Take the next three weeks and force yourself to be with this person in a variety of settings. Just observe. Don't share your concerns with anyone, and definitely don't spread the word to anyone that you're considering getting rid of this person.

If you notice poor performance and rude behavior from this individual, then schedule a private meeting with the person and share your observations. Let the person know that this is not the type of performance or behavior you're looking for. Over the next three weeks, observe the person again several times. If the issues persist, put them in writing and clearly warn the person that they have one more month to turn things around. If at the end of another month, you've seen no consistent improvement, then move to let the person go.

You might think that's totally unrealistic. You might feel that you will develop a reputation as a ruthless manager. My hunch is you won't. Instead your employees will admire the way you dealt with a situation that should have been dealt with a long time ago. However, some employees may be angry. That comes with the territory. Your boss might be angry with you, but remember that you are being held responsible for winning the Management 500. That means treating employees respectfully, which includes dealing honestly and fairly with disastrous employees.

In almost every situation where a manager put off dealing with a disastrous employee, he or she said to me six months later, "I wish I had moved much faster on getting rid of that person. We lost a lot of momentum early on that would have helped our whole team be more successful."

Personal Habits

If you start the first ninety days of the three-year race with the attitude, "I'm just going to have to work 24-7 for the next three months to get everything up and running the right way," then you're putting in motion a short-term solution with a long-term problem. The habits you exhibit during the first three months will very much be the habits you display over the following thirty-three months.

If you ignore physical exercise, personal development, family time, and socializing with friends just to get off to a good start, then you're going to continue to do that over the remainder of the race. Then problems may start coming at you. These problems can range from getting out of shape, wearing down, feeling lonely, burning out, and thinking that no job is worth losing your friends and family. Suddenly the exciting race can become a terrible burden, and you may consider quitting.

Take out a sheet of paper. Write down exactly the way you want the first ninety days to go in non–job-related areas. Make a list of where you want to be in terms of your family life and friendships, and how you want to be physically, spiritually (if you are a spiritually-oriented person then I strongly recommend Joe Gibbs's book, *Racing to Win*,[2] which clearly explains the importance of operating at the intersection of spirituality and business), mentally, emotionally, socially, and financially. As you go through the beginning of the race, refer to that sheet often. Build into your schedule time to keep the non–job-related aspects of your life up to speed. In doing so, you're building habits for the whole race, habits that will keep you fresh and excited about the race ahead.

THE END OF THE BEGINNING

Your first three months constitute the beginning of the race. You are now fully engaged in the challenge of generating significant, sustainable, and profitable growth for three years in a row. What lie ahead are problems to be resolved as well as opportunities to lead, grow, build a stronger team, improve, and take on challenges. This is exciting. This is the race you wanted to be in. You've earned this opportunity. Keep going. Your best days are in front of you.

CHAPTER FOUR

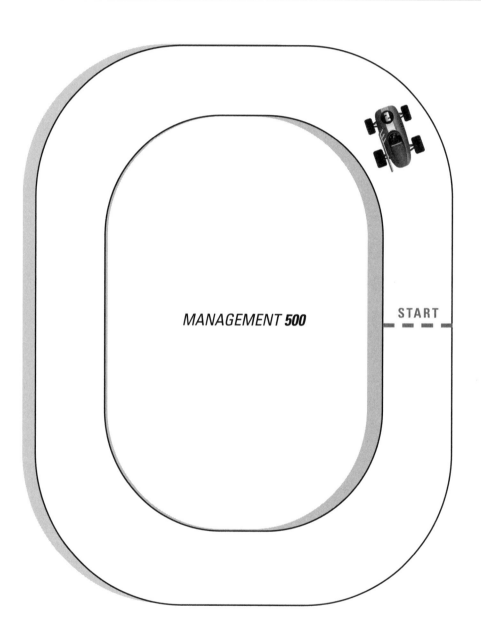

MANAGEMENT 500

START

LEAD THE *WAY*

Richard Petty, Dale Earnhardt Sr., Michael Schumacher, and Jeff Gordon are four of the greatest racecar drivers in history.

Dale Earnhardt Sr. and Richard Petty each won the NASCAR Winston Cup, which is the season-long competition for the championship and now named the NASCAR Sprint Cup, seven times as drivers, making them tied for the most championships ever in the history of NASCAR. Michael Schumacher won the Formula 1 Grand Prix World Championship seven times, which is the most ever in Formula 1 history. Jeff Gordon won the NASCAR Winston Cup four times, which is the third most in NASCAR history, and he is still competing.[1]

THREE KEYS TO LEADERSHIP

These four drivers represent three of the keys to being a successful leader as a business manager.

Every Leadership Style Works, Except One

Richard Petty, known as "The King" to NASCAR fans, is a beloved figure throughout NASCAR racing. His trademark is his accessibility to fans. During his thirty-three-year racing career, he was known to stand with his back to a fence for hours while signing autographs for everyone who asked. His direct, one-to-one relationship with fans played a large role in the eventual extraordinary rise in popularity of NASCAR.

Dale Earnhardt, Sr., was known as "The Intimidator" for his driving style. His car was all black and his objective was to grab the lead as early as possible in the race. He wouldn't hesitate to bump into other cars to move them out of his way. He became one of the most popular drivers in history with fans because of the combination of his wins, swash-buckling driving style, and friendly, down-to-earth sense of humor that had drivers and fans alike laughing. His tragic death on the last lap of the 2001 Daytona 500 created such a stir that many fans still stand during Lap 3 of the Daytona 500 with three fingers raised to honor the driver who drove the #3 car.

Michael Schumacher virtually always kept his emotions in check. His strength as a driver was his ability to stay abnormally calm and composed during the most treacherous parts of a Formula 1 Grand Prix race. He attacked the turns in the track with ferocity going into the turn, in the middle of the turn, and coming out of the turn. Schumacher's extraordinarily high degree of physical fitness was part of his trademark style.

Jeff Gordon is known more as a clinician. His level of preparation in all aspects of getting ready for a race is extraordinary, from studying the various tracks to reviewing every aspect of a race on the Tuesday following the Sunday race. He and the other members of his team study every opportunity to gain fractions of a second at every race. In NASCAR racing the standards for each car are so similar that the difference in performance is created through meticulous preparation. Gordon and his #24 team have been successful because of their exceptional preparation.

Here's my point: these four great racecar drivers were incredibly successful and yet their styles were very different. One of the keys to their success is that each person remained consistent with his style and none of them tried to be someone he wasn't.

The act of influencing others is how you make your mark as a leader. Your style as a leader is the approach you use to influence other people. I've seen every conceivable style, except for one, work very well.

I've seen leaders brag constantly about their own greatness, come across as incredibly arrogant, and essentially put other people down over and over. Amazingly to me, many of these leaders have been extremely effective. I saw one person tell raunchy jokes over and over, and yet this person was very effective as a leader. I'm convinced if I ever did that four armed guardsmen would enter the room, wrap me up in masking tape, put me on their shoulders, and take me out of the room.

I've seen effective loud leaders, quiet leaders, extroverted leaders, introverted leaders, tall leaders, short leaders, male leaders, and female leaders. Success as a leader has nothing to do with personality, gender, race, height, or any other label. The key is to be true to yourself and consistent with your own style.

The only approach I've seen fail every time is the chameleon. A chameleon is a lizard that changes its color to fit the surroundings. The chameleon in business is the manager who changes his or her approach or stance every time a different audience is in the room. This type of "leader" is really a people pleaser, and consequently no one knows what to expect. When people don't know what to expect, they stop being open to that person's influence.

Go for the Win

One thing these four drivers had in common was an incredible capacity to consistently win over an extended period of time. It was the story of these drivers and other great racecar champions like them that inspired me to write this book. I was looking for real-life examples of people who had to move their organizations very fast with great strategies, planning, and execution over a number of years to be considered among the best of the best.

Richard Petty's father, Lee Petty, won the first Daytona 500, which is like the World Series or Super Bowl of NASCAR, in 1959, and was a three-time NASCAR champion. Richard Petty went on to win the Daytona 500 seven times. He won a record number of races (200) and poles (127), and finished in the top ten over 700 times. His

The Process for Honing Your Leadership Style

1. Don't underestimate the importance of honing your own leadership style. If you change your style frequently, you might come across as the dreaded chameleon.

2. Write down seven to ten adjectives that describe your desired leadership approach. For each adjective write down what you can do to act in accordance with that adjective.

3. Look back at the end of each day at your actions and determine where you acted in accordance with your desired leadership style and where you were out of sync.

4. Each day try to make your behaviors more in alignment with your desired approach.

NASCAR Winston Cup championships occurred in 1964, 1967, 1971, 1972, 1974, 1975, and 1979. That means over a period of fifteen years Richard Petty continued to win NASCAR championships.

Clearly Richard Petty learned some valuable lessons from his father. What lessons have you learned from your mentors that you can use today to be an even more effective business manager? Take some time to reflect on those people who went ahead of you and extract some of the key insights you learned from their words and their examples.

Dale Earnhardt Sr. didn't even start racing on a regular basis in NASCAR until he was twenty-seven years old. Imagine an NBA rookie or NFL rookie being twenty-seven. He did win the NASCAR Rookie-of-the-Year award that year, 1979, but he didn't seem destined for greatness considering the late start of his racing career. The reason it took him so long to become a regular NASCAR driver is he simply wasn't given the opportunity. No one with enough financial strength was willing to give him a spot until Rod Osterlund decided to make

Earnhardt Sr. his regular driver in 1979. With that opportunity, he went to work and won the NASCAR Winston Cup in 1980.

If you've spent several years waiting for your opportunity to run a business or manage a profit center, then learn from Dale Earnhardt Sr. He spent nearly ten years in absolute obscurity on the verge of poverty preparing himself for his opportunity. He poured every dime he had into trying to improve his ability to win races.

After his first Winston Cup championship, he then went six more years before his next championship. Some people may have thought he was a one-time wonder, but he persevered for his next run at greatness. He went on to win the NASCAR Winston Cup championship in 1986, 1987, 1990, 1991, 1993, and 1994, with the last championship coming at the age of forty-two.

If you've had a few trying years after an initial success, continue to persevere. Your legacy of greatness may be just ahead of you, but you have to persevere with focus and constant improvement in order to get there.

Michael Schumacher represents the story of winning with two different types of organizations. In 1994 and 1995, Schumacher won the Formula 1 Grand Prix World Championship for Benetton Formula 1 Racing Team. He was only twenty-five years old when he won in 1994, a virtual unknown, and Benetton was the underdog racing organization. Schumacher was then recruited to drive for the long-term powerhouse racing organization, Ferrari Formula 1 Racing Team.

Success did not come easily at Ferrari. Schumacher failed to win the Formula 1 Grand Prix World Championship in 1996, 1997, 1998, and 1999, although he did finish in the top five drivers each year. The pressure was mounting on both Schumacher and Ferrari. Ferrari had not had a driver win the world championship since 1979, and Schumacher was being paid $25 million a year to produce a championship.

Then starting in 2000 Schumacher went on to do what no other driver in history has done: win the Formula 1 Grand Prix World Championship five years in a row. The results were stunning. By the end of his career in 2006, Schumacher had the most world championships, the most Grand Prix victories, the most poles, and the most points in the history of Formula 1 Grand Prix racing.

Have you ever been recruited away from an underdog organization that produced success only to join the top company in an industry and fail to produce great results? If so, be patient, stay calm, work to continually improve, and think of Michael Schumacher as you gradually guide the top company to heights never seen before.

Jeff Gordon joined NASCAR in 1992. In one of the great ironies in sports history, Jeff Gordon's first NASCAR Winston Cup race was also Richard Petty's last. Gordon broke the mold of a NASCAR Winston Cup champion when he won his first championship in 1995.

He was only twenty-four years old, the youngest Winston Cup champion in the modern NASCAR era, and he wasn't from the southeastern United States as so many champions from the past had been. Raised in California and Indiana, he moved to North Carolina when he joined NASCAR. Not only was he an incredibly young champion, but he went on to win the NASCAR Winston Cup in 1997, 1998, and came in second in 1996. By the age of twenty-seven he had three, and nearly four, Winston Cup championships.

If you have a different background than other people at your organization, that's OK. It comes down to performance and results, not where you're from. If you are a young manager, be ready for success. Sometimes amazing results will happen early in your career, but only if you're ready to earn those results. Jeff Gordon was ready.

During 1999, Jeff Gordon lost his long-term crew chief and his entire over-the-wall crew, the group of seven people who work on the car during the pit stops in a race. The 1999 and 2000 seasons were frustrating in terms of results, particularly in comparison to what he and his team had achieved in the previous four years. Then in 2001, Gordon won his fourth Winston Cup.

When you're no longer the bright, young management star and you've had a few years of frustrating results, hang in there. Gather your new team members together and keep searching for ways to add more value to customers. Eventually, you will put yourself in a position to win another championship.

Put the Organization First

Despite their differences in personality, experience, and approach to racing, one thing that Richard Petty, Dale Earnhardt Sr., Michael

Schumacher, and Jeff Gordon had in common is they consistently praised their crew members. When they lost a race, they didn't point their fingers at a mechanic or crew chief. Instead they focused on how the team could be successful going forward. I'll talk more about this characteristic in Chapter 7.

TEN ACTIONS TO LEAD THE WAY IN THE MANAGEMENT 500

You're now at least three months into the three-year race for sustainable, profitable growth. It's time to lay the foundation of leadership that will guide your organization through all of the challenges and opportunities on the track ahead of you. As a business manager, you have a variety of ways in which to provide leadership.

In a professional car race, a great driver and his or her team always look to gain the fractions of a second that will ultimately add up to at least a narrow victory. In business, a great manager always looks for ways, both big and small, to help guide the organization to victory. He or she knows that small, consistent gains will ultimately add up to long-term success. Here are a variety of actions you can take as a business manager to lead the way.

Leadership Action #1: Champion the Least Respected

If members of your organization are showing disrespect for certain employees just because of the department they are in, then you have an opportunity, and in my opinion a responsibility, to step in and provide leadership. I'm not talking about poor performers who demonstrate no desire to improve, be on time, or be prepared. They have earned a lack of respect from their peers. I'm talking about people who are not treated with respect and as credible team members simply because of their function or department.

It's been my experience that the least respected functions are meeting planners, administrative assistants, business researchers, trainers, and human resources.

The Process for Creating Championship Functions

1. Spend one-on-one time with each department head to clarify your respect and expectations for his or her function.

2. Look for specific, observed behaviors that generated solid results.

3. Point out to the entire organization the importance of the person's (or department's) work, the great performance that was delivered, and the specific example of what you are referring to.

4. Repeat for all functions within the organization.

Imagine an organization not being focused on attracting, retaining, and developing the right type of talent to achieve their desired outcomes. Imagine no one coordinating schedules or making sure that the right documents get to the right people at the right time. Imagine having a big meeting with no thought being poured into establishing an agenda, preparing presentations, finding a location, or ordering food. Imagine doing no research on your business activities and the corresponding results or on the market trends you're facing. Imagine sending your employees into sales or operational situations with no preparation.

I know it sounds crazy, but that's what an organization would look like without meeting planners, administrative assistants, business researchers, trainers, or human resources professionals. Once you take the time to see the enormous value these behind-the-scenes contributors make to the overall success of the organization then it's up to you to ensure that everyone in your organization sees the value in these people.

Here's what not to do. Don't stand up at a meeting and say, "I expect the people in operations, sales, and marketing to show more respect to our human resource managers, business researchers, trainers, administrative assistants, and meeting planners. They do important work and they deserve to be treated with respect." That would be a nightmare scenario. Instead I encourage you to meet with individuals from those functions and have one-on-one conversations.

Meeting Planners

For example, in your conversation with the person responsible for meetings, ask what the person's approach will be to making the meeting a valuable experience in terms of effectively improving short-term and long-term results.

See if the person has a strong plan in place for establishing the purpose of the meeting and coordinating the theme, presentations, discussions, entertainment, meals, and location that will support that purpose of the meeting and improve desired business results. If you need to ask follow-up questions or offer practical suggestions on how to improve the impact of the meeting, then offer those, but only after you've heard the person's ideas.

After the meeting, make it a point to let everyone in your organization know how much you value this person and the role of planning effective meetings. In this way, you're subliminally letting everyone know that the role of the meeting planner and the person in that role need to be respected for what is being done.

Administrative Assistants

With the various administrative assistants, be sure to spend some time with each of them during the first ninety days, and then look for examples of the strong work they do. Occasionally ask some of your direct reports for examples of how their administrative assistants add value to their efforts. Then in a public setting let the group know how much you appreciate a specific admin assistant and talk about the specific actions that were so successful.

Too many times admin assistants get swept under the rug of, "Let's give a big hand to all of our administrative assistants in celebrating administrative assistant week," only to never be mentioned again for the rest of the year. Just as you point out great work from individuals in operations, sales, marketing, and finance with specific examples, I encourage you to do the same with your administrative assistants.

Business Researchers

I have seen some internal business researchers treated like royalty and others seemingly forgotten and left in a corner. My suggestion is either use the person's expertise or shut down the position. There's no point in investing in a full-time staff member doing business research if you're not going to be open to input from that person regarding future decisions and direction.

Meet with your business research person twice a month and work to gather insights that are pertinent to the short-term and long-term results of the business. You can ask simple open-ended questions such as, "Based on your research into what drove customers to either buy or not buy from us, what three things do you think had the greatest positive impact and what three things had the greatest negative impact?" Discuss the person's answers and then ask, "How can you best share those insights with the rest of our organization, key business partners, and suppliers?"

In time, your business research person will see that you value his or her research, perspective, and input, and be more willing to share it with you and the rest of the team. Once you have some good examples of how insightful business research affected important business results, highlight the person's impact with the rest of the organization. You can do that via e-mail, webcast, podcast, voicemail, newsletter, large and small group meetings, and so on.

Trainers

It's been my experience that in-house trainers are usually left to themselves to provide training for other employees. There is a certain upside to this approach for the trainers. They gain greater autonomy in developing their curriculum and their method of delivery. The downside is the trainers can feel isolated from the rest of the organization, as though they are running a business outside of the overall organization. Because of a lack of interaction with other department members and senior management, the relationship between the trainers and the other team members can become frayed and even contentious.

Attend some of the training sessions. See the type of training that is being delivered to your employees. Stand up at the end of the training session and publicly recognize the trainer for specific powerful insights that were shared with the attendees. When you go back to your office, send out an e-mail or voicemail letting people know how much you valued attending a specific training session. Ask the trainer to use part of a large meeting to teach something new to the entire organization. This is another step in building up the reputation of less respected departments. Ultimately the goal is to make sure that every department and function is respected for the importance of the role it plays in helping the organization win the three-year race.

Human Resources

The human resources department is perhaps the least respected and most underutilized department in all of business. For the human resources department to be recognized for being a real value-adder to the organization two things must happen: the individuals within the human resources function must perform at a high level, and the business manager must recognize top performances by the human resources department in order for everyone in the organization to understand the importance of the function.

Schedule a meeting twice a month with your HR manager and ask some of the following questions regarding talent management:

- For the type of business we're in and the outcomes we're trying to achieve, what type of talent do we need in this organization in terms of customer interactions, technical knowledge, work ethic, levels of creativity, ability to work with other team members, and so on?

- Which of our employees demonstrate talent in these specific areas?

- How can we enhance the role these individuals play in moving results forward?

- How can we help them take their talent to a higher level?

- Which employees demonstrate none of the talent we need in our organization? How can we help those individuals find employment elsewhere?

- How will we find the type of talent that we need to bring into our organization and how will we recruit those individuals to join us?

- How will we retain a higher percentage of the talent we need?

- How will we develop this new talent when we hire these individuals?

A great HR manager will come to you with these questions and their answers in order to discuss them with you. However, you may need to ask these types of questions to get the point across that you expect human resources to be actively involved in talent management.

As with my other examples, when the HR professionals start to demonstrate behaviors that impact business results (for example, a key hire who revamps operations and improves efficiency levels dramatically), be sure to give some credit both to the new hire and to the HR person who recruited, interviewed, and hired the individual.

Leadership Action #2: Behave with Your Expectations for Others in Mind

Corporate culture is a fancy term that simply means how people throughout the organization consistently behave. As the business manager, you set the standard in terms of how employees will behave and interact with each other. Remember that you don't establish a standard for expected behavior by what you tell others to do. You set it by what you actually do. Whatever behaviors you want consistently demonstrated in your organization need to be first demonstrated consistently by you.

Leadership Action #3: Use Effective Nonverbal Communications

The business managers I've coached have been invariably surprised to learn how much their employees watch them every day. An employee might say to me that the boss looks angry about his presentation, and the boss might say to me she was thinking about her child's soccer game last night. Your employees don't know your internal thoughts. They only know your external behaviors. Read those last two sentences again.

If you look happy when an employee says his parent died, you obviously aren't listening. This contrast between what was said and your nonverbal response can be disturbing to the other person. Be in tune to what is happening around you. Be sure to project the nonverbal messages that you want delivered.

Checking your watch or Blackberry frequently while attending an important presentation sends a lot of nonverbal messages, such as "I can't wait to get out of here," "I've already heard this and I don't need to hear it again," and "I've got so many more important things to do right now." It would be better if you weren't in the room to shout out all of these negative nonverbal messages.

On the other hand, if you patiently listen to an individual or take notes while watching a presentation for the fourth time, you send the nonverbal message that this person is important and this information is important enough for everyone to pay attention to it.

Leadership Action #4: Follow Your Own Rules

This is how you build credibility as a leader, and it's mostly in mundane matters such as meetings. If you tell everyone to be on time for meetings, then you weaken your impact as a leader when you show up ten minutes late. You weaken your impact even further when you tell people you expect them to pay attention and then you bang away on your computer during a presentation.

If one of your rules is that every employee gets two formal evaluations each year, then you have to give your direct reports two formal evaluations each year. Keep a running list of the rules you create for others to follow, and then go through each rule and see if you follow it. Are you behaving with your expectations for others in mind?

Leadership Action #5: Maintain Patience in Crisis

The upside of a crisis is it allows you to demonstrate your leadership capacity to your employees, key business partners, and suppliers. If you start putting the blame on other people and acting indecisive at key junctures, then everyone knows what they are working with in terms of a leader. If you remain calm, communicate clearly, gather input efficiently, and make decisions effectively, then the group knows they are in good hands.

Leadership Action #6: Persist Intelligently in the Face of Failure

When you start competing in the Management 500, you and your group will select certain initiatives to spur revenue growth. If those initiatives fail to deliver immediate results and even reduce revenue, you have a few choices to make. You can jump away from that idea to the next one on the list, or you can analyze what went wrong and implement the original idea again. If you demonstrate an ability to persist even in the midst of initially poor results, you will send a message to the whole organization that perseverance is a characteristic that is valued.

Leadership Action #7: Increase Urgency during Calm Moments

This gets down to the art of leadership: the ability to stay calm in a crisis and create urgency during a calm period. When the results are solid and everything seems to be rolling along smoothly you have a great opportunity to create a sense of urgency. Can you take a positive result and then challenge the group to identify why that positive result was achieved and uncover ways to take the result to an even higher level?

You're guiding the business racecar through the three-year challenge of creating significant, sustainable, and profitable growth. By being OK with a status quo performance level for too long, you may end up sending the message that it's not important to keep improving, and that mindset can really damage long-term results.

Leadership Action #8: Attack Assumptions

Once you're past the first six months in the race, you'll be in a great position to question some of the underlying assumptions that guide daily decisions at your business. If there is an assumption that no teen-ager would buy your company's products and services, ask, "Why is that true? Do we have evidence that teenagers wouldn't benefit from what we sell? Is there anything we could do to our products or services that would make them more pertinent to teenagers? Is there anything we can do differently in marketing to teenagers that would help them see the value of our products and services?"

In the computer industry, it was assumed that no computer company could build a stand-alone retail store that just sold its own computers. Gateway had tried to have its own stores where customers could see their products, order them at the store, and then get them at a later date. That concept failed miserably.

Steve Jobs, CEO of Apple, questioned that assumption. He felt that if customers—and potential customers—had the opportunity to see the Apple products in action alongside experts who could answer their questions, sales would increase. Apple retail stores combined their computers with local know-how and created retail stores that featured the Genius Bar and courses that explained how to use the many features of the computers.[2]

The first Apple retail store opened in May 2001. Within three years the Apple retail stores generated $1 billion in annual sales. By 2006 the stores were producing $1 billion per quarter. Attacking assumptions can be a very profitable action.

If you run a discount shoe store, could you attack the assumption that buyers want shoes and not fashion advice? Could you hire a local fashion designer to give free advice to customers at the shoe store on what outfits to wear with different types of shoes?

Question: What parts of an organization can hold false assumptions?
Answer: Every part.

Here are a variety of assumptions that collapsed when attacked:

Assumptions with Employees

At one private all-boys high school I know, there are no women who work part time or full time in raising money for the school. The underlying assumption is that the all-male alumni would rather talk with men about giving money to the school. Then I met the development group for another all-boys high school that raised more than

The Process for Attacking Assumptions in Your Organization

1. Clarify a specific assumption in your organization and write it down.

2. Ask, "Why do we believe this assumption is true? What evidence do we have? Is there any one thing we could change that would no longer make this assumption true?"

five times as much money as the development team at the first school. Women made up 75 percent of the more successful development team. They operated on the assumption that some alumni preferred to talk with a woman.

Assumptions with Customers and Customer Experiences

It was assumed that only men wanted to watch car races. That is until women started turning out for NASCAR races in huge numbers. It was assumed that customers only wanted low prices at mass retail stores until the Target stores came along and provided a better overall buying experience with wider aisles and less clutter, which generated extraordinary sales.

Assumptions with Products

There was an assumption that people would not watch ballroom dancing or amateur singing on television. That assumption was turned upside down when *Dancing with the Stars* and *American Idol* became rating phenomena. There was an assumption that children wouldn't read long books. That is until the Harry Potter books came along and smashed publishing records.

Assumptions Regarding Method of Sale/Distribution

There was an assumption that customers had to see a computer and order it in a retail store until Michael Dell came along with the idea of selling directly to the customer and creating a customized product for each customer. Several billion dollars in revenue later, Dell had proven that yet another assumption had to be blown up.

Take a look at your business. Study the following list and for each item write down what your organization's underlying assumptions are regarding that item:

- Types of employees we have.

- Types of customers we target.

- Types of products and services we sell.

- Geographic regions we sell into.

- Method of distributing our products and services.

- Method of selling our products and services.

- Price of our products and services.

- Manufacturing of our products and services.

- Cost of manufacturing our products and services.

- Method of marketing our products and services.

- Amount of inventory we need to keep on hand.

- Types of suppliers we work with.

Then take each assumption and ask, "Why is this necessarily true? Do we have any proof? Is there a way to test this assumption?" Of course, don't test twenty assumptions all at once. I'll talk more about narrowing the focus in just a few minutes.

Leadership Action #9: Shake Things Up with a Purpose in Mind

Change for the sake of change is frustrating to everyone. It's frustrating to employees, key business partners, suppliers, and, most importantly, customers. Changing the look of a logo or revamping the org chart or changing prices just so you can say that changes are happening is a waste of time.

However, creating change is an act of leadership. New ideas don't always work, but they may very well open up new possibilities. Thomas Edison was always shaking things up—and often failing spectacularly, not just in light bulbs, but in concrete and phonographs and telephones and on and on.[3] However, even in his failures he found some nuance that could be used in combination with other ideas. Same could be said for Walt Disney and GE and Google and virtually every successful person and organization. Be willing to mix things up.

To shake things up with a purpose in mind, you first must have a clear purpose for your organization. Why does your organization exist? Don't look at your corporate brochure. In clarifying the answer to that simple question, you will build a foundation for making effective future decisions.

The best way that I know of to clarify the purpose of an organization is to bring together the eight to ten top members of the organization and ask them to write down their answers to these questions: "What is the purpose of our organization? Why does it exist?" You can do the same thing for a unit inside of an organization. Simply ask, "Why does this department (or unit) exist? What is its purpose?"

Set aside ninety minutes for discussion and collaboration and establish a reasonably clear statement of purpose. Start by breaking the group into small groups of five people. Let each individual share his or her answers to the questions and then have the small groups discuss the answers for twenty-five minutes. Then the small groups can report out their answer to the questions to each other. Take the next hour to discuss and refine the statement of purpose.

Then send out that statement for further feedback from other employees in the organization. Gather that input, have one more meeting, and put the final revisions on the purpose of the organization. Of course, as the manager of the group, you get to have the final say on the purpose of the organization or business unit. Gather input using a collaborative process, and maintain the capacity to make the final decision.

Now you're ready to shake things up with a purpose in mind. Ask yourself, "What can we do that will stay within our purpose as an organization to mix up what we're doing and generate new levels of innovation, creativity, and customer value?" In implementing your answer to that question you are providing a subtle but powerful act of leadership.

Leadership Action #10: Narrow the Focus and Keep it Narrow

As you act with your expectations for others in mind, attack assumptions, and look for ways to shake up the organization to reenergize creativity and innovation, keep in mind that one of the most important things you can do as a leader is to reduce complexity and avoid process creep.

I've yet to see the organization that will not benefit from a tighter focus. When a business manager keeps the team intact and reduces the number of initiatives and activities, he or she almost always improves morale and productivity. When a business manager creates a dozen changes all at once, he or she almost always reduces morale and productivity.

Of course, the key to generating sustainable, profitable growth is selecting the one or two things that are really going to matter in terms of improving the most important desired business outcomes. It does no good to prune away key activities and be left with a few trivial items that won't affect anything worthwhile. Work with your top employees to tighten your focus.

We're going to look into this concept of reduction a great deal more in Chapter 10 when we discuss innovation. For now, work with your key people to clarify the two most important outcomes you want to improve, the four key items to focus on doing to improve those two outcomes, and the eight items your organization is going to stop doing or spend a lot less time doing.

Listen to all the rationale, which you may want to gather in individual meetings rather than a large group meeting. Consider what you've heard and what you've learned in the previous six months, and then make the difficult decisions as to what the organization will focus on doing and what it will focus on not doing.

Put a chart up in a public area for everyone to see that lists what the organization is focused on doing and on not doing. Then every month review the list to make sure the organization is maintaining a

> **The Process for Narrowing the Focus and Keeping It Narrow**
>
> 1. Identify the two most important business outcomes for your organization to improve in the next six months.
>
> 2. For each outcome, identify the one or two actions that you believe will have the greatest positive impact on improving that outcome.
>
> 3. Identify four to eight activities that will be eliminated or dramatically reduced in the organization.

narrow focus on doing the items it said it would do, and on not doing the items it said it would avoid. It does no good to have a narrow focus if you keep changing the things you're focused on doing and not doing.

Consider each of these ten actions for leading the way, and then select the one or two you think will have the greatest positive impact on guiding your organization to greater success. It's far better for you to do a few leadership actions extremely well than to try to do all ten of them just to say you did them.

CHAPTER *FIVE*

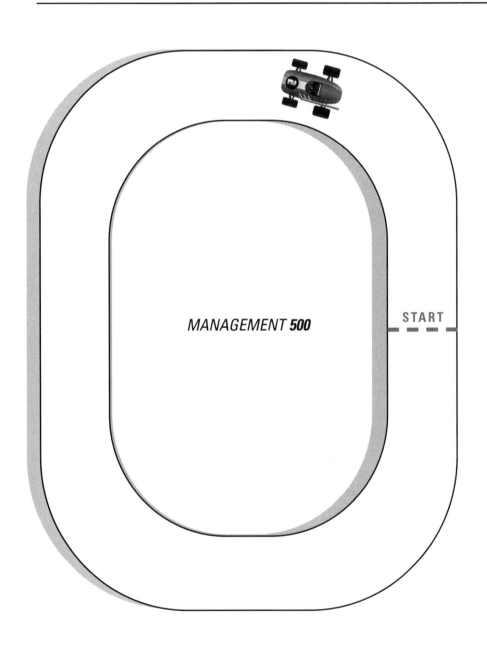

MANAGEMENT *500*

START

DELIVER
PROBLEM-SOLVING-IN-MOTION

Professional racecar drivers do three things: drive their car, work with their team to solve problems, and work with their team to find ways to go faster. Business managers do three things: manage the business, work with their team to solve problems, and work with their team to find ways to grow their business in a profitable way. Essentially, drivers and managers go to work, solve problems, and innovate.

I asked Lee White, president of Toyota Racing Development, USA, how he defined a problem. He told me:

> Any time we're not winning, it's a problem. We're here to win. We're not here just to compete or to be mediocre. I've been in this business for forty years, and I've grown to expect a performance review every Sunday afternoon. There is only one measurement: winning the race. Coming in second place is the same to us as coming in last place. Wherever we finish, the question we ask ourselves is, "Where could we have done better?"
>
> We're an engineering provider and perform our service through a Track Support group for both engine and chassis. This group of engineers travels up and down the pit lane during events and works with each of the racing teams that compete with the Toyota or Lexus

brands. They help predict what benefits or penalties there may be from potential changes to the engine and or vehicle by providing advice to the crew chiefs and teams.

Track Support is supported by the RVE (Race Vehicle Engineering) group, which includes aerodynamics engineers, simulation engineers, chassis design engineers, tire engineers, and software designers back at our home base, which provide information to the teams by communicating through the Track Support group.

We try to turn problems into opportunities. Right now we have 180 TRD associates working for us in California and 45 in North Carolina. That means most of our associates are 2,500 miles away from the epicenter of NASCAR racing. This separation has been characterized by many as a significant problem. Pete Spence, TRD USA Vice President and Technical Director, has turned the three-hour time difference into an advantage.

Since data analysis is fundamental in this business, we try and turn our disparate locations into a three-hour advantage in analyzing data. Our teams do testing in North Carolina, and send the results on a secure website to our engineers in California. Those engineers analyze the data and place their conclusions back on the website so the NC associates and partners have it at the beginning of the next work day. In addition, they place data from testing in California on the website so our partners in North Carolina can also look it over before the California people return to work.[1]

In her book, *One Helluva Ride: How NASCAR Swept the Nation*, Liz Clarke, a sportswriter for *The Washington Post*, described riding with racecar driver Mark Martin for a few laps in the following way:

You might think anyone could strap in a car and race a few laps. Even yourself. How hard could it be? I remember thinking that I might have excelled at this common-man's sport, too, if I had only started early enough.

I had no appreciation for how violent the sensation of the gravitational forces could be. From the moment we pulled out, Martin's feet and legs were in constant motion—clutch, brake, clutch, brake—manipulating the pedals faster than an Irish step dancer. But his upper body was totally relaxed. His right hand guided the steering wheel and manipulated the gear shift—also at a frenzied tempo. But not for one second did he act tense or stressed in the slightest.

Martin flung the racecar around hairpin turns with total commitment. He couldn't see what was around the bend, yet he threw the car forward with no thought that a hazard might be ahead. It was as total a leap of faith as I could imagine.[2]

In many ways, Clarke's brief experience inside an actual racecar parallels the daily life of a business manager. It's hard to have a full appreciation of a "normal" day in the life of a business manager until you ride alongside the person. I've invested about 3,000 hours on site observing managers in the flow of their normal daily situations. Here are some of my observations.

First, there is no such thing as normal. Usually the person has at least twenty-five or thirty e-mails waiting for a response as well as at least a dozen phone messages. Typically the person will attend three to five meetings in the course of the day, some lasting forty-five minutes, others lasting three hours. Many times the manager has to intervene during the meeting and say, "We need to keep this meeting on track, otherwise our time is going to run out and we won't have accomplished our objectives." At other times, the manager will simply need to leave a meeting or skip it altogether just to not be consumed by sitting and listening to reports all day.

In between the scheduled activities for the day are a series of employee and customer requests for availability and answers. Often the employee or customer is very emotional and expects the business manager to listen with great empathy. In addition, the business manager has family responsibilities that need to be inserted in the midst of both the daytime and nighttime business events and travel. Somewhere along the line the manager needs to take the time to prepare for all the meetings, requests, and decisions that need to be made. This is just the normal flow of managing the business.

In addition to the usual work activities, there are two special additions to the manager's role: problem solving and innovation. A business problem is an actual performance that is below the expected performance where the reason for the gap in performance is unknown. A business innovation is the creation of additional value that customers are willing to pay for at a profitable margin to the organization. For now, let's concentrate on solving problems.

When a racecar is expected to go nearly 200 mph and suddenly slows to 70 mph and the driver doesn't know why it happened, that is a problem. When sales are supposed to grow at a rate of 8 percent per year and suddenly slow to 2 percent annual growth and no one knows why the slowdown happened, that is a problem. Notice the race doesn't stop so the driver can go fix his car and the calendar doesn't stop so the manager can uncover ways to grow sales. Problems have to be solved in the course of the race itself, both in car racing and in business.

I asked Geoff Smith, the president of Roush Fenway Racing, how his organization prepares for success both within a given season and for the long term. At the time I asked this question, three of the Roush Fenway drivers, Carl Edwards, Greg Biffle, and Matt Kenseth, were among the final twelve drivers in the NASCAR Sprint Cup Series Chase for the Cup.

Smith said, "Competitive success must be prepared for daily. Each week we are 'tested' to see how well we prepared for that week. Then, after every race we evaluate what happened, both the good and the bad. If something 'bad' happened an adjustment is made and put into motion in every case every time. Every week we also evaluate opportunities to improve based on inputs, including the prior week's performance. Those opportunities determined to be cost beneficial (i.e., performance gain worth the investment) are ordered into motion. Consequently the entire performance machine is being evaluated and adjusted regularly."[3]

How can you take problems your organization faces and turn them into opportunities? The key to success is to solve the problems while staying in motion. You don't have the time to develop a new process for every problem that occurs. You need a process that can be applied efficiently and effectively in the midst of the race. The two best management books I've ever read on problem solving are *The New Rational Manager* by Charles Kepner and Ben Tregoe, and *The Unofficial*

Guide™ *to Power Managing* by Dr. Alan Weiss.[4] Their logical, step-by-step approaches to solving problems provided a strong foundation for the process I've used with clients.

When faced with any business problem, which I have defined as a performance that is less than expected and you don't know why the gap is occurring, here is a process you can use to work toward identifying and solving the problem.

Here is a brief explanation of these aspects of problem solving:

The Process for Delivering Problem-Solving-in-Motion

Clarify the following:

1. Success

2. The Problem

3. The Parameters

4. The Reason

5. The Alternatives

6. The Solution

7. The Prevention

Success

Success is achieving a performance you expected to achieve. Be clear, specific, and reasonable in describing the expected performance. In that way, you will know whether or not you have been successful. If you achieve the expected level of performance, then don't create imaginary problems that will eat up your time and energy.

Pie-in-the-sky aspirations are not expected performances. They are dreams. Dreams are important, but they cannot serve as the basis for uncovering problems. If you don't know what the specific, reasonable performance that is expected, how will you know when you've had a gap between expected and actual performance?

The Problem

A problem is achieving a performance that is less than expected and not knowing the reason for underperformance. If you know the reason why you didn't accomplish what was expected, then you don't have a problem. You simply need to address the known reason. That doesn't mean it's going to be easy, but at least you know what you're trying to resolve. However, if you can't explain why the "poor" performance occurred, then you have a problem. The essence of problem solving is finding the reason why the performance was less than expected and then solving that underlying root cause.

In order to ultimately solve a problem, it is extremely important to clarify the problem in as much detail as you can. Look to answer the following questions: what performance was below expected, where did it happen, when did it happen, and how widespread was it? The more clearly you describe the problem, the better your chances are of finding the root cause.

The Parameters

The parameters are the amount of time, energy, and money you are willing to invest in solving this particular problem. Some problems simply are more important than others. You have to decide how much you're willing to invest to achieve the expected performance. If you invest too much in a trivial problem, you may not have the time, energy, or money to solve the more important problems.

When you are first confronted with a problem, write down the investment you are willing to make as an individual and as an organization to solve the problem. Keep these parameters in mind as you work to solve it. As you get closer to the outer limits of your parameters, be willing to let go of this problem and move on to something else. Too often managers become emotionally invested in solving a particular problem and go way beyond reasonableness in terms of giving their time, energy, and money.

The Reason

The reason is the underlying root cause of the problem that explains why the gap in performance has occurred. The first key to effective problem solving is to answer the question, "Why?" As in, "Why did this below expected performance happen?"

The best way to find the reason for the problem is to compare situations where the expected performance occurred and other situations where it could have occurred but it didn't. Closely examine what was different about the situations. Use your experience and knowledge of the business, customer trends, and other key information along with insights from your employees and suppliers to generate a list of potential reasons why the performance was less than expected in some situations but not in others.

Then test every one of the possible reasons to see if it answers all of the aspects of the problem in terms of what below expected performance actually happened, where it happened, when it happened, and the extent to which it happened.

Once you've landed on the reason that seems to best explain why the problem has occurred, then test it even further to see if it is the root cause. In his book, *The Toyota Way*, Jeffrey Liker explains that Toyota Motor Corporation uses a set of principles to solve problems.

Principle 12 is "Go and see for yourself to thoroughly understand the situation (Genchi Genbutsu)." Principle 13 is "Make decisions slowly by consensus, thoroughly considering all options, and implement decisions rapidly." Principle 14 is "Become a learning organization through relentless reflection (Hansei) and continuous improvement (Kaizen)."[5] As you work to solve problems in your organization, consider using these three proven principles, not only to solve the immediate problem, but also to garner insights for improving future performances.

Another approach I've learned from Toyota is "The Five-Why Analysis." When you have a reason that explains the problem, ask, "Why did that reason occur?" See if you can uncover a more root cause. Then repeat that process four more times. In order to resolve the problem and keep it from reoccurring it's very important that you have identified the true root cause. Asking why five times can help lead you to that underlying cause.

The Alternatives

The alternatives are the variety of ways to attempt to resolve the underlying root cause of the problem and achieve the expected performance. Knowing the root cause of a problem is not a solution in and of itself. You and the other members of your team now need to develop a variety of alternatives to solve that root cause. Each alternative will have pluses and minuses. No matter what alternative you select, it will have consequences. As you sift through each alternative, try to project what consequences will occur in the future.

The Solution

The solution is the alternative you have decided to implement to achieve the expected performance in a sustainable way. Remember: there is no perfect solution. You have to go with the alternative that fits reasonably within your parameters and that you believe will have the best chance of solving the problem in a sustainable way.

Once you've selected a solution for the problem, remain committed to implementing it as well as you can. It does no good to select an alternative only to give it a half-hearted effort and then quickly turn to another possible solution. This is why it's important to try to gain consensus from the group before committing to action. If people don't really buy into this selected solution, they may consciously or subconsciously sabotage the effort. You may not have the ultimate solution to the problem, but you won't know unless you commit to excellent execution within the confines of your parameters.

The Prevention

Once a solution has been implemented and the problem has been solved, the key is to make the necessary changes to prevent this particular problem from occurring in the future. Solving problems cost time, money, and effort. Making adjustments to avoid future problems may generate enormous reservoirs of time, energy, and money that can be invested effectively in running the day-to-day business and creating innovations that will ultimately help the business grow profitably in the future.

A CASE STUDY OF DELIVERING PROBLEM-SOLVING-IN-MOTION

One of the most frequent problems that managers focus on is what they call "the bottom 10 percent." However, as this case study demonstrates, sometimes the problem isn't what it appears to be.

Steve was the national sales manager and said to me, "We will hit our goals if we can just get the bottom 10 percent of our employees to perform better." Then he began to focus all of his attention on the bottom 10 percent of his employees throughout the country. He rode with these individuals on sales calls, sat with them and went over their calendars to make sure they were actually working, and in general micromanaged them into submission. Unfortunately, the performance of the bottom 10 percent didn't improve at all.

Success

I asked Steve how he defined success. He said the expected performance was a national increase in annual sales of 12 percent.

The Problem

Steve said, "Right now our organization is generating an 8 percent increase in annual sales. I know that 90 percent of our sales people are doing between 11 percent and 13 percent, but the bottom 10 percent of our sales force are all doing 3 percent or less. Ten percent of our sales force performs significantly below the other 90 percent in terms of quarterly new sales, and they are killing the rest of the group's results, and I don't know why they are so far below everyone else."

The issue was that Steve didn't clarify the poor performance with enough detail. The first step we took together was for him to answer these questions: Where is the poor performance occurring? In what parts of the country is it happening? When is it happening? Is it during a specific quarter or during a specific time period within the quarters, weeks, or days? How often is it happening? Is it every day or a few days a month or a few weeks a month?

In the end, we found the poorest performing sales people, those in the bottom 10 percent, all worked in three regions in the country. We also found that their poorest performances almost always occurred at the beginning of a quarter. During the first three weeks of each quarter, the revenues produced in these three regions were significantly less than in every other region. This gave us a new definition of the problem: "The bottom 10 percent of our sales people work out of regions A, B, and C and they have their worst performances at the beginning of each quarter, but we don't know why this is happening."

We now had a basis for comparing where the expected performance was happening and where it could have been happening but wasn't. The comparison group consisted of all the other regional offices.

The Parameters

I asked Steve how much time, energy, and money he was willing to invest in solving this problem. He said it was the number-one issue on his agenda. He believed his organization could hit their annual sales goal if he could solve the problem of the bottom 10 percent and get them to be much closer in sales to the rest of the country. He said he was willing to invest one percent of total sales if that's what it took to solve the problem, and that he would dedicate most of the next forty-five days to resolving the problem.

The Reason

I then asked Steve to find out what each regional manager did prior to the end of a given quarter. I wanted to see if there was something different between what was happening in the three regions below expected performance and all of the other regions. In interviewing each of the regional managers, we found that each person did a variety of different things that impacted performance. Trying to find a single reason to explain the problem was like looking for a needle in a haystack.

Then we found something very interesting.

We found out that every regional manager whose sales staff was achieving the desired performance held a meeting with their staff members during the last week of a quarter to talk about the importance of getting off to a good start during the first three weeks of the next quarter. These regional managers shared statistics with their staff members showing how getting off to a good start inevitably led to a strong finish.

However, the three regional managers whose sales people were performing well below the expected results did not conduct such a meeting. Instead their focus at the end of each quarter was on trying to hit the numbers for the quarterly report. Not only that, they then encouraged their staff to relax and enjoy themselves at the beginning of the next quarter as a reward for working so hard.

Boom. Steve now felt that he had clearly identified the reason for the problem. He felt the reason for the poor performance was the difference in the end of the quarter meetings. However, I asked him to do "The Five-Why Analysis" just to make sure he had found the root cause of the problem.

I asked, "Why did the regional managers have different end of the quarter meetings?"

He said, "Because they can run their meetings any way they want and some felt it was important to focus on the next week and others felt it was important to focus on the next quarter."

I asked, "Why can they run their meetings any way they want to?"

He said, "Because I want them to feel autonomous in running their own businesses."

I asked, "Why do you want them to feel autonomous in running their own businesses?"

He said, "Because that way they will perform at a higher level."

I asked, "Why do you believe that complete autonomy will cause people to perform at a higher level?"

He said, "I see the root of the problem. I haven't asked the regional managers to share their best practices. I haven't worked with them to create a collaborative environment where they can maintain their autonomy *and* learn from each other. Consequently, we're ending up with a wide range in actual performances because we have no consistent approach to generating an expected performance. Ultimately, *I'm* the root cause of the problem."

While I assured Steve he was being a little hard on himself, I did congratulate him for his honesty. Rather than focusing on the behaviors of the bottom 10 percent, Steve now saw a different approach to improving the performance of sales people in all the regions.

The Alternatives

We felt we had a good chance to solve the problem. Instead of focusing on the behaviors of the bottom 10 percent of the employees, Steve focused on the three regional managers who had the poorest performers.

His first alternative solution was to send the three regional managers with the underperforming sales people to the meetings at the other regional offices that were held a week before the end of the quarter. However, he decided that would send the wrong message. The problem wasn't with these three regional managers, and he didn't want them singled out.

His next idea was to bring the regional managers together to discuss their ideas for improving a variety of aspects of the business. One item Steve wanted to put on the agenda was, "How to get off to a good start each quarter."

The Solution

Rather than spotlighting the three regional sales managers with the poorest sales, Steve was going to focus on having ideas shared and discussed on a topic that was important to the three regional sales managers. This way the critical issue would be addressed without placing blame on anyone. This critical issue of getting off to a good start was just part of an overall agenda.

The three regional managers with the poor sales then came back to their offices and shared the same information with their employees about the importance of starting the quarter on a strong note. Within two quarters, the performance among the bottom 10 percent of the sales force improved dramatically during the first three weeks of the quarter. With that early momentum, those individuals were able to stay with the rest of the pack throughout the quarter. Consequently, the overall sales force was able to achieve its goal of 12 percent sales growth.

The Prevention

The essential early mistake was not focusing on what made the majority successful. Instead energy was concentrated on what theoretically the poor performers were doing wrong. They weren't doing anything wrong. They simply weren't being given the same level of understanding and preparation as the rest of the sales force. Consequently, they didn't see the importance of starting a quarter strong, inevitably fell behind, and then wasted a lot of time being scolded for being behind. This pattern also didn't do their self-esteem much good, which further hurt their performance over the long run.

Once Steve identified the root cause of the disparate performances, he took steps to keep it from happening again in the future. Instead of treating each regional office as a completely separate business that had no connection to the other regions, he realized that each office did some things extraordinarily well and that those best practices needed to be shared with the other regional managers.

Consequently, once each quarter he identified a trend within his business that needed to be improved. He identified two or three regional managers who were doing extremely well in terms of those outcomes and had those regional managers share their best practices on that particular topic with the other regional managers. In this way, he addressed the root cause of the problem, which was clarified as, "Lack of collaboration between regional sales managers in terms of sharing best practices that are driving sustainable improvement in results."

EIGHT PROBLEM SCENARIOS BUSINESS MANAGERS FACE REGULARLY

Over the past eleven years, I've noticed patterns of problems, and so-called problems, that managers face on a regular basis. Here are eight of those typical scenarios.

Scenario #1: The Problem That Didn't Exist

One common investment of a manager's time is in attempting to solve a problem that doesn't exist. Joe was very upset that Mary, the sales group's star performer who regularly achieved sales numbers that were 15–20 percent better than anyone else in the group, never congratulated him on having a good sales month. He felt Mary was selfish and self-centered. He wanted to know why Mary never shared her best practices with other members of the group. Joe complained frequently to his boss, Tom.

Tom asked me what he could do to solve the problem. I went immediately to The Process for Delivering Problem-Solving-in-Motion.

I asked, "Tom, what is the performance you expect from your group?"

He said, "Our objective is to achieve an 8 percent growth in sales this year."

I further asked, "What is your current growth in sales?"

He said, "We're at 11.25 percent right now."

I then asked, "Are you losing good sales people because of Mary?"

He said, "Not at all. Mary's a little quiet, and I wish she spent more time teaching others how to sell more, but she's pleasant to be around. She's just very quiet and introverted."

I said, "Tom, you do not have a problem. Your desired performance is better than expected, and nothing is happening that will hurt the sustainability of your group. What you have is a basic human situation. Joe wants Mary to congratulate him more often. That's not part of her job. She doesn't have to do that. Let Joe know it's not Mary's responsibility to congratulate anyone, and then don't waste any more time on this situation. Put your energy where it matters most."

Situations like the one with Joe, Mary, and Tom happen many times. The first step in solving a problem is to see if there really is a problem. You only have a problem if the actual performance is below the expected performance and you don't know why the gap exists. In this scenario, there is no problem so don't worry about it.

Scenario #2: The Problem of Unrealistic Expectations

In order to solve a problem, you have to be able to compare instances where the expected performance is occurring with instances where it is not occurring. However, if the expected performance has never occurred anywhere in any organization at any time, then you have no basis of comparison for uncovering why the current performance is below the expected performance.

I know that makes sense logically, but it often doesn't make sense emotionally to managers. Some managers will set a goal of increasing revenue by 25 percent next year even though no region in their business and no organization in their industry has ever increased sales by more than 12 percent in one year.

Then at the midway point in the year many of these managers begin to obsess over how to solve the performance problems. At which point I say, "There is no performance problem. There's an expectation problem. You selected an expected performance that had no basis for being expected. Therefore, there's no way for us to find a comparison between those people who are achieving it and those who aren't because no one is achieving it. Don't waste any more time on worrying about a problem. Instead focus on improving the current level of performance to whatever the highest level of improved performance in one year that has actually occurred in the industry."

Scenario #3: The Problem with Getting Emotional about Results

One thing I've noticed over the past eleven years is that many times when people get results that are better than they expected to achieve, they get pretty excited. When it happens twice in a row, they get really excited. When they achieve results that are better than they expected to achieve three times in a row, they become flat out irrationally optimistic and act as though the good times are never going to end.

On the other hand, many times I've noticed that when people achieve results that are less than they expected to achieve, they're a little bummed out. When it happens two times in a row, they're really bummed out. When they achieve results that are less than they expected three times in a row, they become irrationally pessimistic and act as though the bad times are never going to end.

I refer to this as "The Psychology of Results." Alan Greenspan, the former Chairman of the Federal Reserve, wrote about this phenomenon in his extremely thought-provoking book, *The Age of Turbulence: Adventures in a New World*.

He wrote:

> Economists cannot avoid being students of human nature, particularly of exuberance and fear. Exuberance is a celebration of life. We have to perceive life as enjoyable to sustain it. Regrettably, a surge of exuberance sometimes also causes people to reach beyond the possible; when reality strikes home, exuberance turns to fear. Fear is an automatic response in all of us to threats to our deepest of all inbred propensities, our will to live. It is also the basis of many of our economic responses, the risk aversion that limits our willingness to invest and to trade and induces us to disengage from markets.[6]

Not only do individuals get overly emotional about results, but the media can compound the problem by crafting compelling stories that feed on this irrational optimism or pessimism. The job of the media is to tell compelling stories based on facts that attract readers and viewers. Consequently, during economic hard times, you will find daily stories about how bad the economy has become. Rather than getting caught up emotionally in these stories, it's very important for business managers to stay rational.

When my daughter, Sarah, turned nine years old she had five of her girlfriends sleep over at our house. After we made pizzas, played games, ate cake and ice cream, and opened presents, my wife, Barb, and I finally got the girls down to sleep on our family room floor. About twenty-five minutes later, Sarah came running upstairs and she said to us, "Mom and Dad, we hear keys rattling downstairs and we don't know what's going on."

Barb and I went downstairs and we checked the windows and the doors and underneath the furniture for burglars. Then we finally realized that the noise was the zippers on the sleeping bags. The more nervous the girls became, the louder the zippers got, and the louder the zippers got, the more nervous the girls became. We needed to stay logical in dealing with the noise the girls heard, and business managers need to stay rational with results and not become overly emotional about the media stories.

This same phenomenon of getting emotional over results happens inside businesses as well. Mark was a results-driven executive. The reason I know that is because the very first time I met him, he said, "Dan, I'm a results-driven executive."

I said, "That's good because I think the role of an executive is to make decisions that improve results in a sustainable way." Mark then went on to tell me four more times in the next forty-five minutes that he was a results-driven executive.

I asked, "Mark, what do you mean by a results-driven executive?"

He said, "At the beginning of every quarter we set a goal. At the end of the quarter if we achieve or exceed our goal, then we celebrate. If we don't hit the goal, then I come down pretty hard on people. Sometimes I lay people off just to get the point across that we have to hit our goals."

I said, "Mark, how much money are you leaving on the table using that approach?"

He said, "What are you talking about? I'm not leaving any money on the table with this approach. Sometimes our results are up and down, but that's true throughout the industry."

I said, "Well, how much time and energy are your employees wasting worrying about results that they could be using to actually improve results?"

He said, "People have told me it can be pretty nerve-racking to work for me, but, hey, that's business."

I said, "Mark, you're only answering the first two questions. There are five more questions to answer regarding results."

He said, "What are you talking about? What five questions?"

I said, "Well, you're just answering the questions, 'What was our goal?' and 'What did we achieve?' But there are five more questions to answer. They are, 'What did we do to try to achieve the goal?' 'What worked well and why did it work well?' 'What did not work well and why did it not work well?' 'What lessons have we learned or relearned during this time period?' and 'What will we do the same and what will we do differently going forward in order to improve results?'"

Mark looked at me and said, "Dan, I don't want to drive our business looking in the rearview mirror all the time."

I said, "I don't want you to look in the rearview mirror all of the time either. However, if you don't pause and reflect on what has happened, then you're just repeating the same approach over and over again."

Over the next three years, Mark still celebrated successes and still came down hard on people when goals were not met. However, every thirty days he brought together his top eight managers, and together they invested an hour in discussing their answers to all seven questions. Over those three years, his organization's business results steadily improved in an industry where results constantly fluctuated.

Scenario #4: The Bottom 90 Percent Problem

In the case study earlier, I wrote about the bottom 10 percent. That is the area that most managers seem to focus on. However, the opposite situation can also be a problem, although it rarely gets the same attention. If 90 percent of your employees are performing at one level and 10 percent of them are performing at a substantially higher level, then you have a problem, which can be clarified as, "90 percent of our employees are performing dramatically below our top 10 percent and we don't know why."

By posing this situation as a problem, you can then begin to apply The Process for Delivering Problem-Solving-in-Motion in the same way it was applied in the case study. Compare the habits of the individuals who are in the top 10 percent with those individuals who could be in the top 10 percent but are not. What reasons could explain why 90 percent of the employees are not performing at the same level as the top 10 percent? Don't see the top 10 percent as an inexplicable phenomenon. Instead search logically for ways to improve the performance of the bottom 90 percent.

Scenario #5: The Problem Organization

I've seen entire organizations that performed dramatically below their competition. Since no one in their organization was performing at a high level, they had no examples to compare themselves with. At least they had no examples inside their organizations. However, they had plenty of them in other organizations in their industry.

If your whole organization is performing well below the industry standard, then don't just give up. Look for what great performers are doing in other companies inside your industry. If you can't find a great performer in your industry then look at other industries. You need a point of comparison to see what the great performer does differently than a person who could be achieving a great performance but isn't.

Scenario #6: The Same Old, Same Old Problem

Jill was a successful operations manager. She was known for her steady approach to business. She stayed calm and kept everyone else calm. She spoke often about focusing on the basics of the business and not trying to be fancy. When she was promoted to regional manager, she became very popular with her employees. Rather than making their lives more complicated, she stayed focused on simplifying their lives. For the first two years, her region achieved great results and Jill was applauded at the national meetings by her boss.

Then something odd happened. Jill's business results started to stagnate. She was now in the middle of the pack in terms of sales. In her fourth year, Jill's region fell near the bottom of the national results. She had fallen into the trap of always doing the same things in the same way, which meant her region was not providing any additional value for customers to consider.

Consequently, the competition began to take away her business. A lack of innovation is a real problem, especially if you are getting poor results and you don't why it is happening. Jill's work ethic and motivation remained high, but her ability to create innovations for customers remained low. Eventually, she was demoted back to running operations.

While maintaining focus is a business driver, that focus can't always remain on the same approach. We'll discuss the importance of innovation in Chapter 10, but for now I'll just say that staying with an approach that worked with customers in the past does not mean it will automatically continue to work in the future. You have to consider new possibilities for creating value for customers.

Scenario #7: The Love of New Ideas Problem

Kurt had the opposite problem. He simply loved to create new ideas for generating revenue. It didn't bother him at all that the ideas had no connection to each other or to the business strategy. If he had an idea that he thought would generate some sales, he implemented it. This approach seemed exciting at first. The creative juices were flowing throughout the business. That is, until reality set in.

The marketing department found itself overextended in trying to market all of these ideas effectively. To make matters worse, the operations team simply could not execute all of the details of all of the new products. In the beginning, customers liked the new variety, but then they became very angry over the lack of quality and customer service. New ideas are only truly innovative if customers buy them at a profitable margin to the business. They are not innovative if they turn customers off and damage profitable growth.

Although Kurt was very creative, he suffered from a complete lack of focus. He turned this around by applying his creativity within a few very focused areas. In doing so, the products and services offered by his organization stayed within a much tighter framework, but became much more valuable to the customers, and he achieved sustainable, profitable growth.

Scenario #8: The Loss of Dignity Problem

The ultimate problem for a racecar team is the death of a driver during a race and not knowing why it happened. After the death of Dale

Earnhardt Sr. and a number of other drivers in 2001, NASCAR dramatically stepped up efforts to improve the safety of the drivers.

The ultimate problem for a business manager is completely losing his or her dignity and not knowing why it happened. Personal dignity is the degree to which a person feels he or she is in control of decisions affecting his or her future. When people feel they have completely lost their dignity, they are unable to function effectively. This is true for both men and women at all age levels and at all salary levels.

Business managers who have lost their dignity can still do tasks, but they are unable to make decisions. Consequently, they must be told what to do at every step in the running of the business. Business managers can't operate this way. They must have their dignity in order to move forward effectively.

Business managers rarely die on the job, but I've seen many of them who lost their dignity in order to "please the boss." It's critically important that you always maintain your ability to do what you think is the right thing to do in a given situation, even if it means losing your job. If you lose your job and retain your dignity, you can live to race again in the Management 500. If you give up your dignity to keep your job, then you've lost your ability to win the current race and any future race. Before you follow through with a decision, be certain that it's a decision you can live with regardless of the results it produces.

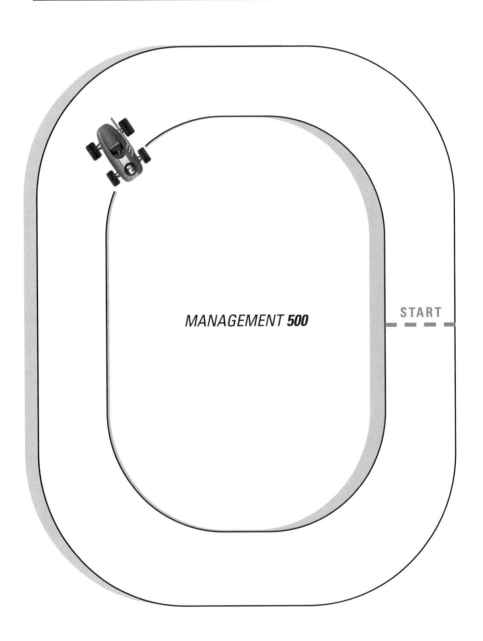

CHAPTER SIX

MANAGEMENT *500*

START

USE PIT STOPS
WISELY

"Time for what I hope is the last pit stop of the race. . . . Every second off the track is costing us 100 yards. . . . Now for the most stressful part of the race: changing tires and adding fuel in 12 seconds, while I keep the engine running. I relax my cramped, bleeding fingers from their steel grip on the steering wheel for the first time in 33 laps. . . . I move my fatigued shoulders to loosen the tension that comes from being stuck in one position for over three hours.[1]"
  —**Bobby Unser, winner of the Indianapolis 500 in 1968, 1975, and 1981, describing a pit stop**

Executing an effective pit stop is as much a part of winning a car race as selecting the right crew chief, building a great car, or maneuvering efficiently through turns in the track. Pit stops encompass strategy, teamwork, communication, planning, and flexibility. Knowing when to take a pit stop, being able to operate efficiently coming into and going out of the stop, taking care of the car effectively during the stop, and knowing when not to stop are all part of winning a race. During a pit stop a driver can relax for a few seconds, get fresh tires, gain new fuel, and come out ready to go after the victory.

Racecar drivers need to sustain a high level of concentration for long periods of time. A one-second lapse in concentration and discipline can cause a serious wreck or even death. In business, a manager needs to sustain a high level of concentration for long periods of time. A lapse in concentration and discipline can cost millions of dollars, if not billions of dollars, in missed sales opportunities, lawsuits, and operational breakdowns.

Drivers need pit stops to refuel, reenergize, and renew their performance. The same is true for business managers. A pit stop for a business manager means taking a break from the act of managing the business. You have to see the benefits of stopping, plan ahead accordingly, and be flexible in when you take a pit stop in order to optimize each one. You also have to be ready to take an emergency pit stop when the situation truly calls for one.

WHY BUSINESS MANAGERS NEED PIT STOPS

Here are some of the main reasons why I've seen managers take a pit stop and get away from their businesses for awhile.

Enhanced Energy and Better Physical Conditioning

Cars need fuel and fresh tires to keep going at a winning pace. You need to eat and drink properly in order to keep going at an extraordinary pace. Look at every breakfast, lunch, and dinner the same way a racecar driver looks at a pit stop. Your meals are your opportunity to pour in effective fuel that can help you sustain a great performance. Choose your fuel carefully. It will dramatically affect your performance as you move through the day.

You also need a fresh set of tires that can sustain the incredible impact of going 200 miles per hour. Your tires are your overall physical fitness. Do you have the stamina to stay focused and disciplined in stressful business situations? Does your performance wane dramatically in the last few hours of each work day? By getting away from your business and using a portion of that time to enhance your physical conditioning, you will be able to sustain great management performance for longer periods of time.

During a pit stop, a car may need more work done on it than just having the tires changed and the fuel tank filled up. As a manager, you may need a pit stop for a knee surgery, an annual physical, or an appointment with a physical therapist. Ignoring those can cause a physical blowout later in the year.

Better Perspective

When a racecar driver is a few inches away from another car going 200 mph, he or she can lose sight of the bigger picture. Avoiding a collision now can allow him or her to win later on. By giving his or her mind a rest during a pit stop, a driver can come back on to the track with a clearer sense of the plan he or she needs to adhere to in order to win.

By getting away from your business for a few hours or days, you can come back to the business with a fresher, broader perspective of what to do and how to do it. This is just one way that downtime can accelerate management performance.

New Insights

By getting away from your business, you will increase your chances of seeing other businesses with fresh eyes. In doing so, you may find insights from inside and outside your industry that you would not have known about otherwise, insights that can be used successfully in your business.

Greater Sense of Purpose

By investing some of your time, talent, and energy in your community or in local or national not-for-profit organizations, you may gain a greater sense of purpose in your work. It may help you realize that your business is just one piece of a much bigger puzzle. This might help you realize a greater sense of purpose in how you can make a difference in the world through the work you do.

Stronger Relationships with Family Members

In the end, isn't life about relationships? Time with family members is not a pit stop. Relationships are what life is all about. The Management 500 is a subset of your life, not the other way around. By taking breaks from your work to exercise and read and do fun activities, you can enhance the energy you have for your family.

By making sure that your family remains the umbrella in your life and work remains just one subset of that umbrella, you can keep work in perspective. This can actually improve your performance at work.

Attending your child's soccer game or going on a date with your spouse are not pit stops. That's real life. But if you're worn out from the work day and have no energy left when you get home, then you're endangering the most important part of life: relationships with family members. In all likelihood, you won't get as much time with family members as you pour into your work. And that makes every hour with family members just that much more important.

THE RANGE OF PIT STOPS

As a business manager, you have a range of opportunities to step away from the act of managing your business and enhance the quality of what you bring to the business race. Here are a variety of potential pit stops you can take and some suggestions for each one.

Social Pit Stops

A racecar driver earning millions of dollars a year goes at top speed for a relatively few hours a week. If that's the case, why do business managers think it's a good idea to work sixty hours a week or more? I don't think it is a good idea. Actually, I think it's a terrible idea. You're a social being. You need to socialize with other folks.

Pull out your calendar. What do you have scheduled that's just a social event in the next thirty days? Do you have any downtime planned where you're just going to have fun with other adults? If you have a social event with people from work, then keep it social. Talk about hobbies and kids and events, but don't talk about work. I know that's easier said than done, but if you're not careful every waking hour can be about work and that can burn you out.

Be creative in building social events. If you enjoy the opera, set a date and get there. If you enjoy sports, then watch a game with a bunch of friends. I'm not talking about watching your kids play or dance or perform. That's family time. That's critically important, but that's not what I'm talking about here. I'm talking about making sure you get some social time in with other adults.

Physical Pit Stops

Essentially, you need energy to perform at a level high enough to generate sustainable, profitable growth for three years in a row. Getting physically drained is a surefire way to have one great year followed by two lousy years.

Physical pit stops are really about building healthy habits. Basically, there are three factors involved in sustaining health: how you exercise and how often you exercise, what you eat and drink, and how much rest you get. Let's go through each of these separately.

I encourage you to schedule a minimum of three workouts a week. Block out ninety minutes three times a week on your calendar. Then do something that gets your heart pounding and strengthens your body. Hop on a treadmill and put in three to six miles, take an aerobics class, or play tennis, racquetball, or basketball. These physical pit stops will increase your energy and make you more effective.

If you have a ton of lousy food available at work, then take a pit stop from the bad food and eat something healthy. Visualize yourself pouring valuable fuel into your body. Look at what you eat and ask your self, "Will this diet help me win the Management 500 over the next three years?" What you eat and drink largely determines your weight and your energy level. Do you realistically have the energy you need to guide your organization to a higher level? You don't have to be fanatical to carve out the time to eat healthy food and drink nourishing fluids.

The most overlooked aspect of health is proper rest. I've met many managers who worked out daily, ate well, and looked exhausted.

They loaded up their schedules with work, community, and home responsibilities and burned the candle at both ends and in the middle. They constantly talked about how they were always busy and very tired. They were operating on five hours of sleep or less each night.

You need sleep. Please read that one again.

Here's a suggestion. If you have early morning meetings and dinner meetings and late responsibilities at home, then take a nap every day. You read that right. I know you're a successful manager with tons of responsibilities. That's exactly why I'm recommending you take a nap every day. Thirty minutes of rest in the middle of the afternoon can keep you sharp through the rest of the day.

Look at your weekly calendar, and carve out three nights where you're going to get seven to eight hours of sleep. You may not be able to do that every night, but three nights a week is a lot better than none. If you have a dinner event and won't get to bed until midnight, then don't plan a 6 AM meeting the next day. Remember that your organization needs you around for the long term, not just the banquet.

Mental Pit Stops

A business is basically a flow of ideas. The ideas your organization decides to focus on implementing are what ultimately define your business. What separates two businesses are the selection of ideas they have chosen to implement and the effectiveness with which they implement those ideas.

As a manager, two of the most important facets you bring to your organization are the quality of your ideas and your ability to sift through other people's ideas to see what would be effective in moving the business forward in a sustainable and profitable manner. In order to focus on ideas, you need to sometimes stop actively managing the business and carve out a pit stop to sit and reflect.

Schedule an hour a week to just think. Go to a place where no one knows you. Take out a blank sheet of paper. Then go through each of the ideas you've heard other people—including suppliers, customers, employees, and competitors—share about how to grow the business profitably. Consider each idea and see if there's a way to combine the idea with another idea that might make for a more powerful concept.

Don't go into the hour with an expectation for a deliverable. Just think about other people's suggestions and consider them.

Alan Greenspan said that when he was the Chairman of the Federal Reserve he set aside time every day just to reflect on all the information that he had reviewed. He also said that many days he took a hot bath with a legal pad and a waterproof pen. This allowed him to calmly think through the various financial situations the United States faced at that moment. He saw the importance of thinking and the economic power of ideas.

He wrote, "If you compare the dollar value of the gross domestic product of all goods and services produced in 2006 with the GDP in 1946, after adjusting for inflation, the GDP of the country is seven times larger. The weight of the inputs of materials required to produce the 2006 output, however, is only modestly greater than was required to produce the 1946 output. This means that almost all of the real value-added increases in our output reflect the embodiment of ideas."[2]

Another part of a mental pit stop is reading. If your knowledge of business is confined to what you already know, you may be missing out on some key ideas that could generate significant growth. Carve out some time each week to read. One good idea can help you generate extraordinary results, but you have to occasionally pull your management car off the track in order to find those ideas.

Emotional Pit Stops

You're human. Consequently, you have emotions. You can become excited, angry, frustrated, curious, nervous, or overwhelmed. To keep your emotions from bubbling over in the wrong way at the wrong time, I encourage you to build in a pit stop that allows you to keep your emotions under control. One action I recommend a lot is for managers to leave the building and go for a walk every day. If it's cold out, put on a coat. If it's raining, put on a raincoat. By getting outside, I think you'll enhance your ability to consciously gain control of your emotions and then fifteen minutes later be able to go back inside in a better frame of mind. A fifteen-minute pit stop outside can make all the difference in the next two hours on the inside.

Financial Pit Stops

Since folks worry about money as much as they do about almost anything else, I encourage you to take an occasional pit stop and find out exactly where you and your family stand financially. At least once a quarter get a very firm grip on your bills, your investment portfolio, your foreseeable income, and the financial decisions you need to make.

Knowing bad news is better than knowing no news. With knowledge you can make decisions on how to improve the future. Operating in the dark will only increase your anxiety level or lead to decisions that may make your situation even worse in the future. If it turns out that you have good financial news, then that will help you sleep better at night.

Community Pit Stops

For my money, there's nothing more enriching than a community pit stop. When you give your time, talent, and energy pro bono to a community nonprofit organization, you'll always get more back than you give.

Every year I give somewhere in the neighborhood of seventy presentations that consist of keynotes and general sessions at national conferences, luncheon speeches, after-dinner speeches, and seminars. I have given speeches in virtually every market in the United States. However, the one speech I'll never forget was the keynote speech I gave at the graduation ceremonies for J.E.T. (Jobs and Employment Training) for St. Patrick's Center in my hometown of St. Louis, Missouri. St. Patrick's Center provides hope for homeless people. It's an organization that helps homeless people find a place to stay, food to eat, and training to get a job.

The nine people I spoke to were probably more excited about graduating than the graduates at Harvard University. They had just completed a twelve-week class on basic computer programs and other job-related skills. Even though this program is for men and women, there were all women that day. These women ranged in age from roughly thirty-five to fifty years old. Many were single moms who had been living on the streets of St. Louis.

I talked about some of the exact same ideas that I do in my keynote addresses to executives and entrepreneurs. I talked about how to maintain daily enthusiasm and strengthen self-confidence and focus on contributing to other people. The difference between this speech and all the other ones I've given is that this time I had to work very hard to keep myself from crying.

I looked into the eyes of these nine women and I saw incredible winners. I saw people who weren't going to allow life's greatest obstacles to keep them from succeeding. They were by far the most inspiring group of people I've ever met. Before the ceremony, I had a chance to meet each of these women. I know every one of their names. I don't have to look them up. They are emblazoned on my mind.

Do you see the extraordinary impact that community pit stops can have on your life? Find an organization or two that you can contribute some of your time, talent, and energy to. Give them the best you have to give, and watch as your sense of purpose grows and grows.

THE FREQUENCY OF PIT STOPS

There are short pit stops and long pit stops. Some happen daily and some happen once or twice a year. Obviously if you take too many pit stops from managing the business, you won't win the Management 500. On the other hand, if you don't ever take a pit stop you won't win the race either. I don't know what the right balance of pit stops is for you, but it's somewhere between none of the time and all of the time. Find the right frequency for you. Here are some thoughts on the timing of pit stops.

Daily Pit Stops

I recommend you clear your head for at least twenty minutes every day. Between work responsibilities and home responsibilities, you have a steady demand on your time and energy. If you don't clear your head at least once a day, it won't be too many days before you get overwhelmed. Find something you enjoy doing and do it. For example, I like to read the sports page. I've done it since I was a kid. There's no real business benefit to reading the sports page. I almost never use anything in it, but it gives my mind a rest. What can you do? Work on a crossword puzzle, read a fun novel, watch a favorite television show, go for a walk . . . whatever you enjoy.

Weekly Pit Stops

I definitely encourage you to get away from your boss, peers, employees, customers, and suppliers for an hour a week to think. Go to a coffee shop where you won't run into anyone you know. Write down an open-ended question that you want to answer on a notepad or the latest e-pad—or even on a paper napkin. This can be about a business outcome or issue or it can be about a personal outcome or issue that you feel needs attention.

Invest thirty-five minutes in answering that question from a variety of perspectives. Then take ten minutes to combine ideas together to make even better ideas. Then, during the last fifteen minutes, select your best idea and develop an action plan on how you can move that idea into action. Then go back to the office and to the job of managing the business.

I also encourage you to schedule at least three physical pit stops a week to exercise.

Monthly Pit Stops

Every month I encourage you to set aside an hour to answer the questions on the next page.

I have yet to find a simpler and more productive set of questions for improving performance month after month.

Quarterly Pit Stops

As you look out to the next quarter I encourage you to schedule at least four consecutive days where you get completely away from work. Obviously some quarters you will go away for far longer than that, but

The Process for Raising the Bar

1. What were your three most important goals for the past month?

2. What did you actually achieve in the past month?

3. What did you do to try to achieve those goals?

4. What did you do that worked well and why did it work well?

5. What did you do that did not work well and why did it not work well?

6. What lessons did you learn or relearn in the past month?

7. What will you do the same and what will you do differently to make next month better than last month?

I think it's really important every quarter to get at least four consecutive days away from the job of managing the business. I've seen managers brag about saving up their vacation days for years only to produce mediocre results quarter after quarter. It's not how long you go without a break that matters. It's how long you sustain a continuous improvement in results that matters.

Semiannual Pit Stops

Six months is one-sixth of the Management 500. It's very important to pause every six months and ask yourself, "Am I on the right path to win this race? Am I guiding this organization in the most effective way for us to collectively achieve sustainable, profitable growth? What should I keep doing and what should I stop doing? What else should I be doing? Am I being there for my family members in the way that I think is the right way to be there for them? How do they feel about this? Am I taking care of myself mentally, emotionally, physically, socially, and financially?" Don't let six months go by without carving out half a day to reflect on how everything is going.

Annual Pit Stops

A year is an important milestone. It's time to extend the pit stop concept to the important people in your life: your family members, your best friends, and your key employees. Set up time with each group to discuss what has happened over the past year and what adjustments, if any, need to be made for the year ahead.

With your family I suggest you ask each person what they want the year ahead to look like and what you can do to help them make that a reality. What activities do they want to be involved in, what support do they need from you, and how can you work together to make it happen?

With your best friends, carve out a day or two to have some fun and reflect on the past year and the year ahead. For the past nineteen years I've gone on what we call Dream Weekend with my two great high school friends, Jeff Hutchison and Mike Feder. Every year we go to some city for fun and games. We also carve out seven or eight hours to discuss the past year and the upcoming year. We talk about what went well and what didn't go well, and then we discuss what we hope to achieve in the next year. Then we give each other honest feedback to consider.

With your business, conduct a business physical. When you get your annual physical from the doctor, you get a report on what to keep doing, what to stop doing, and what to start doing. Do the same thing for your business. Work with your top team members to identify which business processes to keep using, which ones to eliminate, and which ones to add in order to improve performance.

STRATEGIC PIT STOPS

In the course of an auto race, pit stops represent crucial strategic decisions. Drivers and their crew chiefs are constantly trying to figure out how many pit stops they should plan on taking, at what points in the race they should take those pit stops, and under what conditions they should take a pit stop and should not take a pit stop. Some very famous races have been won when drivers and crew chiefs decided to skip a final pit stop and go for the victory. Of course, that's highly risky, since the car may run out of fuel or have a tire blow out because a pit stop was eliminated.

As you look out over the days, weeks, months, quarters, and years ahead of you, think strategically about the type of pit stops you want to take and when you want to take them. For example, think about your business team. As you look at the calendar, when do you think your team members will experience the greatest job-related stress? Could you plan a team pit stop that would allow the group to get away from their work for a day or so? Could you schedule a fun event for them, or give them an additional paid holiday to be with their families?

Look at your own schedule for the next year. Do you see times where you might get overstressed? Could you strategically place a vacation on your calendar, or at the very least keep an eye on your calendar so that four days of travel are followed by a day working at home?

Pit stops of all types are very important. The idea is to use them wisely. Rather than going three weeks without a pit stop and then trying to cram them all in during one week, I encourage you to think through the types of pit stops you want to implement and when you want to implement them. Then place those on your calendar. At the very least keep them top of mind so you deploy your pit stops as effectively as any other resource you have for winning the Management 500.

EMERGENCY PIT STOPS

When a driver blows out a tire or ruins an engine, he or she has no choice. The car must be brought in for a pit stop. This wasn't a scheduled stop, but that doesn't matter. The stop needs to happen.

There are times when you have to step away from the act of managing your business. Be aware of these red flags that automatically bring drivers into the pit stops, or sometimes just a complete stop. If your health or the health of a family member becomes endangered, walk away from work and trust that the organization you've built can carry on successfully without you for the time being. Don't be a so-called hero and pretend that you're so important that the business can't survive without you. If you're that great a manager, trust me, the business will be able to survive.

If you suffer a nervous breakdown, it's okay. It's happened to lots of folks over the years. Take the time to take care of yourself. You just allowed yourself to become overheated and exhausted. You probably just tried too hard. Take the time to get away from the work. If the stress caused you to become addicted to drugs or alcohol, then check yourself in for rehab.

Be okay with that. As with any other meaningful objective, trying to win the Management 500 can be very challenging. You're human. You may have messed up, and not taken care of yourself. Be okay with taking a prolonged pit stop and getting yourself and your situation back in racing condition. Three years is a long time. You can still come back and win the race for three years of consecutive, sustainable, and profitable growth—but not if you ignore emergencies.

PIT STOPS CREATE NEW BEGINNINGS

When a driver comes out of a pit stop, he or she is reenergized, refueled, and refocused on winning the race. As you look at the remainder of the three years in the Management 500, notice that every pit stop offers a new beginning. However, each of these new beginnings offers a unique advantage over the original beginning of the race. The difference is that with each new beginning you go forward with the knowledge you've gained since the beginning of the race.

If you never take a pit stop, you are essentially racing with the knowledge you had at the beginning of the race. You're also continuing to race with a diminished physical and emotional capacity. By occasionally pausing, you not only go forward with enhanced knowledge, but also with greater energy and more effective emotions. You still have a long way to go before the end of the race. Take your pit stops seriously, make the most of them, and then go forward each time with a higher level of effectiveness as a manager.

CHAPTER SEVEN

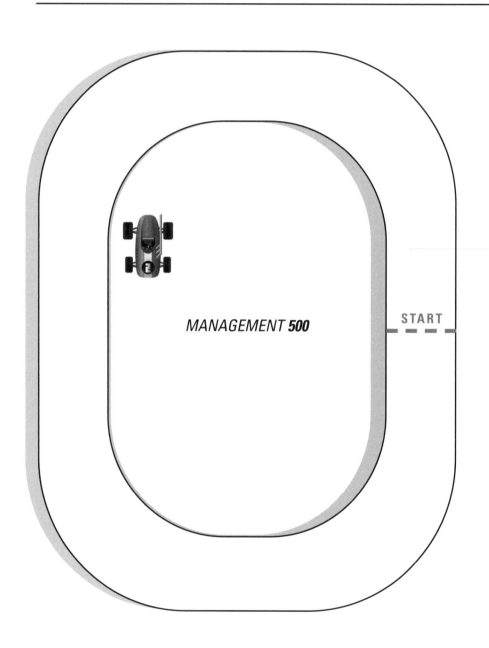

MANAGEMENT *500*

START

CREATE CREW
EXCELLENCE

"A good driver is important; a good car is important; a good crew chief is important; and a competent and motivated crew is important. This is a team sport where car, driver, and crew are linked. . . . All the pieces have to come together, and all the players have to gel to take the checkered flag on Sunday.'"
—**Jeff Gordon, four-time NASCAR Winston Cup Champion**

The greatest myth in all of professional auto racing is that the driver wins the race. That's not even close to true. It's the combination of the driver, the car, the crew chief, the over-the-wall crew that works on the car during the pit stop, the crew members who take care of the car at the shop, the mechanics and engineers who design and build the car, and a host of other people who ultimately guide the car to victory.

Other than the driver, the crew chief gets most of the credit for a successful race. The crew chief is the day-to-day manager of the race team, oversees the mechanics and the crew, and is responsible for the setup of the car and any changes that are made during the race weekend. The driver is primarily in contact with the crew chief in describing information about how the car is handling.

In racecar driving, there are also unsung crew members such as the crew members changing the tires, who have to operate with extraordinary precision and efficiency; the catch can man, who is an over-the-wall crew member who holds a special container to collect fuel overflow during pit stops; the gasman, who is an over-the-wall member of the crew responsible for filling the fuel cell during pit stops; and the engine specialist, who is in charge of preparing the engines at the shop, and fine-tuning the engines at the track.[2]

And there are extended team members who impact performance as well, including the sponsors, the owners, the car designer and manufacturer, the car chief, the team manager, and many other folks behind the scenes.

Pit crews will practice for incredibly long periods of time in order to reduce the time it takes to change tires and refuel a car in order to save a few seconds at a pit stop. This purposeful, prepared teamwork is ultimately what allows a great driver to succeed. In his memoir, *Jeff Gordon: Racing Back to the Front*, Jeff Gordon mentioned several times how he would meet with his crew chief and members to let them know how important each of them was to the overall success of the team.

As a business manager, you will accomplish almost nothing by yourself. You don't have the time or the expertise to design and produce products and services, sell them to customers, deliver them in a timely fashion, and provide ongoing maintenance and problem solving. In other words, you're not going to win the Management 500 by yourself. The greatest myth in all of business is that the manager achieves great results.

When great results are achieved over an extended period of time, it is always because of the combined efforts of individual performers who pulled together to generate those results.

BUILD A TEAM, NOT A FOCUS GROUP

In any activity, a team is a group of individuals who support one another toward achieving a meaningful purpose. Unfortunately, many business groups operate more like focus groups where each person shows up at a meeting, offers their opinion, gets a free lunch, receives a paycheck, and goes home. Focus groups are valuable for providing perspective on a product or service, but they are not effective in working together to improve the product or service. As a business manager, building great teamwork is one of the essentials to driving sustainable, profitable growth for three years in a row.

In their book, *Toyota Talent*, Jeffrey Liker and David Meier wrote, "What Toyota has been able to do is gather competent and trainable people from around the world and, with considerable time and effort, develop high levels of talent within the masses. It is not a few star performers who make up a strong team. It is a collection of many players with good capability working in unison that makes an exceptional team."[3]

Over the past twenty-three years of working with teams of all types, I've seen six steps emerge as being the most essential.

The Process for Creating Crew Excellence

1. Establish the purpose of your crew.

2. Strengthen the format of your crew.

3. Develop crew members with your purpose in mind.

4. Recruit crew members with your purpose in mind.

5. Define winning.

6. Stimulate crew connections for breakthrough results.

These six steps are each critical to creating crew excellence in your organization. I'll go through them one at a time to add greater texture and explanation.

Establish the Purpose of Your Crew

Whether it's a department or a cross-functional team, the basic question is, "Why does this group exist? What is our purpose?" Unless the members of the group know the purpose and believe in the purpose, you have a zero percent chance of success in building a great team.

Hitting a specific number is about achieving a goal. Fulfilling a purpose is about satisfying the soul. Good teams win the race and feel satisfied. Great teams focus on winning the race and fulfilling their purpose. They know each race is merely a point in time on the long-term journey toward fulfilling their purpose, which can never be fully realized.

Both are very important. Hitting a number, whether it's in sales or customer retention or bottom-line profits, is important. Numbers provide the basis for raises and promotions and future career opportunities. Measurable goals are important and I'll talk more about achieving goals in a few pages, but for now I want to talk about the soul.

Members of a group want to feel they are doing something special, something worthwhile, and something that matters in the world. Steve Jobs calls this putting a "ding in the universe." For all the talk about Steve Jobs being difficult to work for and being an extreme micromanager, he has built three extraordinary teams: the team that built the Macintosh computer, the team that built the iPod, and the team that ran Pixar, which ultimately became the primary team that runs Disney-Pixar Animation Studio.

In each case, Jobs got his teams to focus on an incredible purpose. The purpose of each team was different, but they were all compelling. Steve Jobs said, "Unless you have a lot of passion about this, you're not going to survive. You're going to give it up. So you've got to have an idea or a problem or a wrong that you want to right that you're passionate about: otherwise you're not going to have the perseverance to stick it through. I think that's half the battle right there."[4]

After you've spent time getting to know the members of your group and your suppliers and customers and the situation your organization is facing, you're ready to bring the group together to discuss the real essence of why they do what they do. I suggest you bring together anywhere from eight to twenty key members of the team. Then ask someone outside of the group to facilitate a discussion. I suggest the facilitator hand out a sheet of paper to each person with these words printed on it, "Why does this group exist? What is the purpose of this group?"

Notice I'm recommending that you as the business manager not tell the group its purpose for existence. Instead I suggest you become a member of the discussion in establishing the purpose of the group. In doing so, you will allow the purpose to bubble up from the discussions among the group members. As the top executive in the group you can put your finishing touches on the statement of purpose, but if you start the meeting by telling the group their purpose for existence, then it's not their purpose, it's your purpose. That's not about reaching the soul. It's about being a dictator.

The other reason why I suggest you not tell the group its reason for existence is that there is a very good chance you might be gone from the group someday. You might get promoted, transferred, or leave the organization. If the members of the group don't feel ownership of the purpose for the group's existence, then the teamwork may fall apart when you leave.

In Formula 1 racing, there have been two titans over the past sixty years: Ferrari and McLaren. The Ferrari Formula 1 Racing Team has won fifteen Formula 1 Grand Prix World Championships and the McLaren Formula 1 Racing Team has won twelve.

In 1965, a highly successful twenty-eight-year-old driver named Bruce McLaren decided to start his own Formula 1 racing team, which would bear his name and begin racing in the 1966 season. In those early days, Bruce McLaren brought on a young car designer named Robin Herd and a young lawyer named Tommy Mayer to help manage the team.[5] From the beginning, the McLaren Formula 1 Racing Team was focused on the purpose of building an extraordinary racecar organization.

Tragically, Bruce McLaren was killed during a test run on June 2, 1970.

The purpose of the McLaren Formula 1 Racing Team could have died along with Bruce McLaren. The organization had not won a world championship yet, and the members simply could have gone their separate ways to get on with their careers and their lives.

Instead something rather extraordinary happened. The members pulled together even tighter than before. Their determination to fulfill their purpose held the group together. They maintained their name and went on to win the Formula 1 Grand Prix World Championship in 1974, 1976, 1984, 1985, 1986, 1988, 1989, 1990, 1991, 1998, 1999, and 2008. Does your group have a purpose strong enough to win twelve championships after you leave the group?

When everyone in your group has had a chance to write down their answers regarding the purpose of the group, the facilitator can then randomly divide up the group into small groups of five to six people. In those small groups, each person gets the chance to share what he or she sees as the purpose of the group. Each individual gets to talk about why the group exists. Then within each small group the members discuss their answers and arrive at a common statement of purpose. Then each small group reports to the other small groups their collective answer.

At this point, the facilitator can simply say, "Now that we've heard all the statements of purpose from each of the small groups, who would like to take a crack at summarizing what you've just heard into a single statement of purpose?" This is where the clay starts to turn into a great sculpture. A person simply states the purpose of the group in a conversational manner. The facilitator writes the words on a flipchart pad.

Then the facilitator can say, "I would like for each of you to feel free to raise your hand and let us know what you want us to add or subtract from this statement and why you feel that way." As each person shares his or her thoughts with additions and subtractions, the facilitator keeps a running list of what to add and subtract on two other flipchart pads.

After a reasonable amount of discussion, the facilitator takes a crack at summarizing the statement into one for the group to further discuss. Notice the group is crafting the purpose of why it exists, not the facilitator or you. You can put your comments in just like anyone else, but the facilitator should treat you the same way all the others are treated.

There is a reason behind all this back-and-forth discussion. Not only are the members of the group establishing why the group exists, but they are also developing the ability to collaborate with one another. This skill of collaboration will be critically important as the group moves forward in supporting one another to fulfill its purpose.

Overall, I suggest an initial meeting of at most two hours to discuss the purpose of the group. After the first meeting, have the facilitator type up a first draft of the purpose of the group and send it to everyone for them to consider. Wait a day or two and reconvene the group for further discussion on why it exists. Gather additional thoughts, consider those ideas, and move toward final resolution.

As the manager of the group, you will put the finishing touches on the final wording of the statement of purpose of the group, but those finishing touches shouldn't be a complete revamping of what the group came up with. If you disagreed with the purpose that the group was landing on, you should have said something while the statement was being crafted so they could respond to your comments. If you dramatically change the purpose of the group when you go off by yourself, then you have defeated the whole point of the creation of the statement, which was to gain emotional buy-in from the members of the group for the long term.

In the end, I encourage you to land on a very simple statement that can be explained conversationally in the hallway. Purpose statements like, "We exist so our customers get treated like real people," or "Our purpose is to make sure that children have long-term, good health," or "We're here to democratize great clothes" are simple, inspiring statements that clarify why a group has been assembled. When you know why your group exists it makes it much easier to know who to bring into the group, what areas to focus their development on, and what constitutes a breakthrough result.

Before you sign off on the purpose of the group, ask each person one more time, "Is this purpose something that will really touch you each day or does it just feel like words on a piece of paper to you? If it's not strong enough for you, what would make it more powerful for you?" Invest the time it takes to craft a purpose worthy of bringing out the best in people.

Strengthen the Format of Your Crew

The format of the team is how people work together. Are they contentious with one another and openly blast one another's ideas? Are they consensus-driven, where the group politely discusses ideas until they craft one that they can all agree upon? As a business manager, you are going to largely impact the format of the team.

Again, I suggest you ask for input during the early days of forming a team to achieve a three-year goal. Even if you've been with these folks for several years, I still encourage you to ask this question, "How will we work together to fulfill this purpose?" You may want to ask someone else to facilitate the discussion so you can just be a member of the group.

Different car racing teams have different formats. In some cases, the driver talks only with the crew chief and in other cases the driver spends a lot of time with the mechanics to discuss the details of the car. Some drivers, such as Jeff Gordon, are also owners of the team, while others are rookies who have not built up a strong reputation with the other team members yet.

Remember that a team is a group of individuals who support one another toward achieving a meaningful purpose. Having a great purpose with no clear idea on how members are supposed to work together is an exercise in futility. By having the members of the group discuss how to best work together to fulfill the purpose, you may very likely gain insights that you wouldn't have thought of on your own.

As you move forward, attempt to turn this team format into a consistent approach, but not an inflexible one. If the members of the group act toward one another in a consistent manner, then new members will be able to quickly see how this particular team behaves. In that way, the new person can decide if this is a group he or she wants to be a part of. On the other hand, don't make the approaches so rigid that an individual can't develop a new way of interacting with a teammate that creates value for the other person and for the customers.

Develop Crew Members with Your Purpose in Mind

Start with the individuals in your organization right now. Don't denigrate them with comments to yourself like, "How can I win with idiots like this around?" Instead focus on questions like, "In order to fulfill our purpose at a very high level, what skills and experience do our team members need?" Then determine the current level of skill and experience that your current employees possess.

There are only two ways to enhance the skill and experience level in your organization: develop your current employees and hire new employees. If current employees have real passion for the purpose of the group, work well with the other members of the group in creating and delivering value to customers, and have a desire to improve, start with them in terms of developing their skills and experiences. In some cases, you might have to clean house and recruit an all-new team, but I encourage you to look at that as the last possible resort.

Professional development is a double-edged sword. On the one hand, it is critically important in terms of generating sustainable, profitable growth for three years in a row. Your employees are the ones who create and deliver value to customers. As they grow in competence and add more value to customers, the more your business results will improve.

On the other hand, more time seems to be wasted in so-called professional development activities such as training sessions, conferences, mentoring programs, and working with outside consultants than all the other activities combined. Far too often people leave a professional development session with no idea of what they were supposed to have gained from the time they invested.

The primary problem isn't with lack of development but with lack of purposeful development. Purposeful development is an intervention where the employee leaves the session better prepared to help the group fulfill its purpose. Effective development can occur in a number of ways including but not limited to practical classroom application, computer courses, simulation, and on-the-job training with a guide.

One of my favorite examples of purposeful training using simulation is how Toyota teaches its employees to spray-paint a car. Toyota clearly is about creating cars of incredibly high quality at reasonable costs for consumers. The quality of the paint job is critical to the success in fulfilling their purpose. At their paint center, employees practice spray-painting on a two-way mirror, which has a video camera behind it to record every moment that the employee is spraying the paint. The employee can then watch the video, see the patterns they were using, and make adjustments to improve the quality of the paint.[6]

Of course, you can't provide every training moment for all of your employees. What you can do is to work to instill a mindset of purposeful development throughout your organization or group. Whenever you provide a development session for any group of employees, clarify the connection between the session and the purpose of the group. And don't make this an unrealistic stretch where people leave wondering where the connection was.

For example, if the purpose of your group is to provide unparalleled customer service, then taking five members of your team to lunch at the local Ritz-Carlton Hotel can be a very purposeful development session. On the other hand, if the purpose of your group is reducing downtime at a factory, then just taking people out to lunch at a Ritz-Carlton because you enjoy the food there might be considered a waste of time and money.

The Process for Purposeful Development of Your Group

1. Highlight the purpose of your group.

2. Explain the development intervention your group is about to attend and how it can support your group's purpose.

3. After the development experience, discuss with the attendees what has been learned and how it can be applied to fulfilling the purpose of your group.

4. Follow up with the individuals in your group within two weeks to discuss what is working well in applying what was learned from the development session and what is not working well. In that way, adjustments can be made to enhance the applicability of the development session.

Ultimately, great teams fulfill meaningful purposes, but great team members are not ready-made. These individuals need to be developed in order to optimize the chances of the group getting ever closer to fulfilling its purpose. Focus on delivering purposeful development both for your current employees and for those individuals you add to your group in the future.

Recruit Crew Members with Your Purpose in Mind

In a nutshell, I encourage you to develop an incredibly strict and serious hiring approach. Don't hope that someone will just work out. In steps one and two, you invested a lot of your energy and time and that of your team members toward clarifying why the group exists and how people are expected to interact with each other. In step three you focused on developing your current employees to support the reason why the group exists. With that foundation in place, it's now equally important to find team members who can truly help the group fulfill its purpose and work with the other members in an effective way.

If you pour in a minimum effort during the hiring process and end up with people who add very little toward fulfilling the purpose of the group or who simply can't work with the other members of the group, then you've created a massive problem. A poor hire can take the attention of the group off of the group's purpose and focus it on the drama of dealing with a person who shouldn't be there.

One of the most important roles you have as a business manager is to add people who will truly contribute special value toward fulfilling the purpose, and likewise, remove team members who genuinely hurt the team's chances of success. This important role becomes particularly excruciating when it is obvious that certain well-liked, hard-working, and long-term employees simply are not going to help the group fulfill its purpose.

In these situations, the key is to work very hard to help the individual find another job within the organization or with another organization where he or she is a better fit. However, the greatest responsibility you have is to your team—and that includes assembling the absolutely best team you can.

In *Toyota Talent*, authors Liker and Meier wrote, "The truth is that Toyota does like to start with good people who possess the capability to become exceptional employees. The people whom Toyota selects must have the capacity and desire to learn."[7] The surest way to get let go at Toyota is repeated unexcused absences. In order to demonstrate the capacity to learn, you have to be there to learn.

Look at every approach your organization or group currently uses to attract new team members. Are you sending the right message in order to attract the type of employees that you really want in your group? Are you generating enough possible employees to select from in order to find the real gems you need for future success? The stronger the pool of talent you have to select from for your team, the better your chances of success will be in selecting the right new employees.

Be absolutely rigorous about defining the types of employees you need in your group. Obviously you don't want everyone to have exactly the same talent and the same personality. For the different roles within your group, write down the skills, behaviors, and attitudes you're looking for. Ask for input from your best team members on what they look for in new team members. Work with your best team members to develop interview questions, role plays, and case studies that will help determine if this new person is a good fit for your team.

Before you add any new member to your group, ask yourself, "Will this person help us become more effective in fulfilling our purpose?" and "Will this person be effective within the format of our team?" If you are not absolutely convinced that you can say yes to both questions, then don't hire the person.

The people you feed into your organization will largely determine whether or not you win the Management 500. Don't rely solely on your human resources department or your department heads. You are the person responsible for the success of the team, and you should spend time with every candidate who is being considered as an addition to the team.

Define Winning

Winning is the achievement of a specific, measurable goal. For a professional racecar driver, the ultimate goal may be to win the Formula 1 Grand Prix World Championship, the NASCAR Sprint Cup, or the Indianapolis 500. However, there can be a number of other specific, measurable goals to be won such as qualifying for the pole position, driving the fastest lap in the race, or finishing a race in the top five.

Purpose statements are powerful in spurring people on to greater heights, but they are very difficult to measure in terms of actual success. To say your company wants to democratize great clothes is one thing, but knowing whether or not you are making progress toward fulfilling that purpose is another thing. Racecar drivers and their crews measure everything they can: the time it takes to change a tire and fill a fuel tank, the actual time it takes to finish each lap on every track they compete on, the number of sponsors who stay with the team and the number they've lost, and on and on. As much as possible is measured, and those measurements help the racing team decide what to do to improve results in the future.

To win the Management 500 your organization has to achieve significant profitable growth for three years in a row. That is a big specific measurable goal. Within that goal there are many other measurable goals that will help you determine if you are winning or losing. You can measure profits on a quarterly basis. You can measure sales on a daily basis. You can measure number of sales calls made, and you can measure percentage of revenue growth each quarter.

There are an endless number of things you can measure in your organization. Measurements are another form of a double-edged sword. If you don't measure anything, then you don't really know if you're making progress toward the long-term goal. If you measure too many things, you can spend all of the combined time and energy in your organization measuring activities and results and not achieving anything.

While I can't tell you exactly what to measure in your organization, I can offer a suggestion. Pull together the top members of your team and ask them this question: "What are the most important items for us to measure to determine whether or not we are generating significant, sustainable, and profitable growth?"

Obviously the first starting point is for your group to define what "significant" growth means. If your industry is barreling along at 18 percent annual growth, then 4 percent may not be considered a very good performance at all. On the other hand, if the industry's growth has been flat, then 4 percent might be considered significant. Your group might want to up the ante, then, and say, "If we're not achieving 8 percent annual growth, then we need to reinvent ourselves and create a new path for our future that will deliver the growth we want."

As the members of the group begin to identify various items to measure, post all of their answers on a series of flipchart sheets so everyone can see them. At this stage, you're trying to generate every possible important measurement to consider. Obvious ones might include sales, costs, and profits. Less obvious measurements might include "percentage of revenues from our top five customers" or "percentage of sales from our top five sales people."

If too much of your business is wrapped up in a single client or single salesperson, you might be in a lot of trouble if that person moves on. A new goal might be to diversify your client base or to grow sales among the bottom 80 percent of the sales force.

Once you've gathered all of the possible measurements, then the key is to whittle them back to the crucial measurements. As you consider each measurement, have the group answer this question, "If we don't know the answer to this measurement, will we still be able to make wise decisions to generate significant and sustainable growth over the next three years?" Really challenge the group to let go of superficial measurements or misleading measurements.

For example, is the number of cold calls to prospective clients really the best measurement for your organization? In some organizations, the best sales reps aren't making any cold calls. These successful sales people focus all of their attention on delivering great value and great customer service, and build their sales through referrals. By measuring cold calls, you might be emphasizing an activity that really isn't the most effective in generating sales growth.

Once you've narrowed down the items that will be measured in your organization, then make a very big deal about those items. Remind all employees about the purpose of the organization or the group, and the specific ways in which progress will be measured. I've seen companies create road maps, thermometers, and charts that hang in their employee cafeteria, announcing the actual progress for each specific, measurable outcome they are pursuing.

At the end of the day, employees want a sense of whether they are collectively winning or losing—but don't just stop there. Use the actual results as the basis for determining what to do in the future. For each result, I encourage you to use The Raising My Bar Process I provided earlier on a monthly basis, in order to raise the performance toward winning the ultimate goal.

Stimulate Crew Connections for Breakthrough Results

It's not about you.

What your team achieves will largely happen without you being present. The bosses I've observed who felt they had to be in on every discussion and have the final say on every decision were the ones who were the least successful. The bosses who demonstrated trust in the people they placed on their teams were the ones who achieved the best sustainable results.

Once you have worked with your initial team members to establish the purpose of the group, have worked with the group to establish how the members will work together, have focused on developing and recruiting employees to continually improve the team, and have clarified the measurable outcomes that define winning, you need to be willing to stay out of the way. In some ways, that's the hardest part of management: to be comfortable with letting the members of the great team you have brought together and developed work without you to generate great results.

As you step back from active involvement with the team members, I suggest you do two things: encourage unusual combinations and be patient with the payoff. Encourage the members of your team to go out to lunch at least once a month with someone outside of their department. Create the expectation that individuals will spend time getting to know people outside of their daily work group. Then be patient in letting these new relationships grow to the point where new ideas and better results emerge.

In 1980, NASCAR race team owner Rod Osterlund created an unusual combination in teaming an unusually old second-year driver, twenty-nine-year-old Dale Earnhardt Sr., with an unusually young crew chief, twenty-year-old Doug Richert, who was from California. A combination like this had never happened before in NASCAR history.[8]

Osterlund said, "I had confidence in Richert. I thought he was ready."

Richert said, "I never thought about being young. There was too much to do. I just wanted to keep everything going the way it had gone."

By the end of 1980, Earnhardt and Richert won the Winston Cup, making Dale Earnhardt Sr. the first driver in NASCAR history to win Rookie-of-the-Year one year and the Winston Cup the next year.

I asked Lee White, president of Toyota Racing Development, USA, how it builds effective teamwork with drivers and racing teams when Toyota works with multiple drivers and multiple racing teams in NASCAR where they are all competing to win the same race. He said:

> There are a couple of things to keep in mind. No other manufacturer has a relationship like ours with the racing teams since no other manufacturer has a TRD. We don't use the "checkbook model" where a car manufacturer writes a check to a racing team and then the team is responsible for doing all of their own engineering support. We consider this process to be flawed since no team is going to share any gains or improvements with competitors. It has typically been characterized by spending large amounts of support funding which resulted in duplication of effort and waste.
>
> We are here to help everyone who uses a Toyota car or Lexus product to win the race. We treat everyone the same way. We have an open book policy as much as possible within the constraints and challenges of free competition between the teams and by also respecting budgetary constraints.
>
> One of the ways we try to achieve this goal is to distribute a spreadsheet to every one of the teams that use our products. For each race, we ask the crew chief and the driver several questions about the performance of the engine and chassis relative to the competition. We then take their answers and incorporate them into our work for improving the performance of the racecars. If appropriate, we share all of the information we can with each of our drivers and teams.
>
> Sometimes when we learn something confidential from one of

our teams or drivers, we keep that confidential. We won't violate the confidentiality of certain information. We never want to break the trust we have with any of our drivers or teams. However, as much as we can, we provide information to everyone associated with Toyota so they can have the best chance possible to win each race. As long as the rising tide improves the performance of all our teams, we feel we've done our job.

Here's an example of how it works. During the first year we competed in the NASCAR Sprint Cup Series, we struggled with the power curve of the engine. We had one of the most powerful engines at peak rpm but we were down 50 horsepower in the low- to mid-range rpm. We had it backwards. The most important place for the driver to have power is in the mid range, as the best way to achieve a quick lap time is to have the quickest acceleration from the center of each corner to mid straightaway. In the second year we changed our approach and built the engines so the driver had significantly more power coming out of the corners in the track and the results that season speak for themselves.

Teamwork is really about surrounding yourself with quality people because like most businesses it's really all about the associates and partners. Unlike IndyCar and Formula 1 racing, which are almost completely engineering exercises, NASCAR is so different. There is zero data accumulation equipment on the race vehicle during a race so you are 100 percent dependent on the communication and information-sharing skills between the drivers and crew chiefs.

Chemistry is critical in NASCAR. Fifty percent of success in NASCAR is the quality of the driver and the relationship between the driver and the crew chief. For example, it's so much fun to watch the relationship grow day by day between Kyle Busch and his Joe Gibbs Racing crew chief, Steve Addington. From listening to the crew chief/driver conversations, we try to learn how we can add more value to them. The question we ask ourselves for each driver is, "What can we do to help this particular driver and team win?"

Our challenge is to try and figure out the answer to that question and then provide solutions to the problem. Of course then the whole thing is dependant on the team and driver to have the trust and confidence in TRD to take advantage of our offered solutions. Building that trust is a slow and tedious process in itself.[9]

Are there unusual combinations in your organization that you could encourage to happen? Could you combine your best marketing person with your best operations person and send them on a three-day trip together to study the industry? Could you connect a crafty veteran with a hot-shot new star on an important project to see what they might produce?

As you assemble these unusual combinations of team members, just set them up and step back. Don't try to micromanage the interaction or predict the exact results that will come out of these small group efforts. Just maintain faith that talented, hardworking people with complementary skills and a common sense of purpose will achieve something remarkable.

TEAM REMINDERS

Back in the introduction, I wrote about my philosophy of embracing simplicity and avoiding process creep. This is as true for team building as for any other topic in this book. The steps are few and simple: establish a purpose, decide how to work together, develop people with the purpose in mind, recruit new members with the purpose in mind, define winning, and stimulate unusual crew connections.

Teams drive results, not individuals. Check your ego at the door, and build a great team that can sustain excellent performance for three consecutive years.

CHAPTER EIGHT

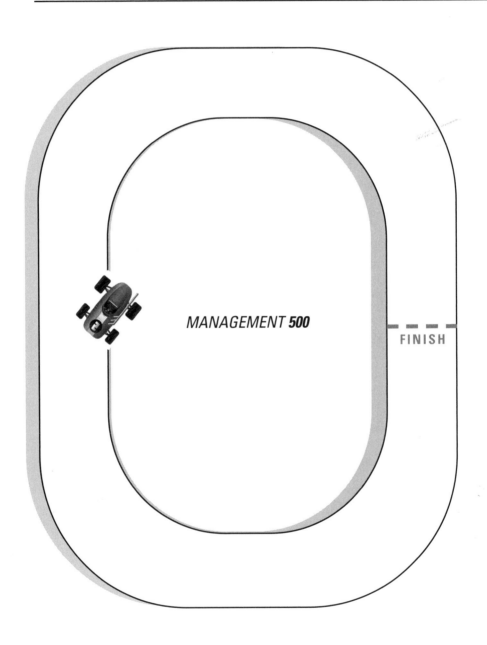

MANAGEMENT 500

FINISH

DESIGN YOUR
STRATEGY TO WIN

A business strategy describes an organization and guides the future decisions regarding the organization.

In 1958 at the age of twenty-one, Roger Penske began his career as a professional racecar driver.[1] By the age of twenty-seven in 1964, Penske had won 51 of the 130 races he entered while driving fourteen different cars in seven different categories. By any definition, he was a highly successful driver.

In 1959 at the age of nineteen, Mario Andretti won twenty feature races in a 1948 Hudson Hornet in local stock car competitions.[2] From 1960 to 1964, Andretti proved his racecar driving prowess in sprint cars and midget cars, and was on his way to bigger challenges in the world of auto racing.

And that is when one of the most intriguing strategic intersections in the history of professional auto racing occurred.

At the end of 1964, Roger Penske decided to leave his life as a racecar driver behind and enter his life as a full-time businessman in owning a car dealership and becoming a racing team owner. He turned down the opportunity to do a test drive for Clint Brawner and his chief mechanic, Jim McGee, in one of Al Dean's USAC IndyCars. Brawner and McGee turned instead to Mario Andretti. Roger Penske focused on building a business, and Mario Andretti focused on becoming a great driver.

Roger Penske went on to build a company that would employ 38,000 employees, own 300 car dealerships, generate $17 billion in annual revenues, include highly successful NASCAR and IRL and ALMS racing teams, and have a nationally recognizable fleet of yellow trucks traveling across America.

Mario Andretti went on to win a Formula 1 Grand Prix World Championship, the Indianapolis 500, the Daytona 500, and three United States Auto Club (USAC) IndyCar championships, and a Championship Auto Racing Teams (CART) IndyCar championship. In 2000, the Associated Press and *RACER* magazine named him "Driver of the Century" and he was inducted into the International Motorsports Hall of Fame.

In 1964 each man had made a decision. Roger Penske was given an opportunity to buy a car dealership, and he decided to change his organization's strategy. Instead of building an organization for him to win races, he built an organization to sell cars and help other people win races. His strategy guided the future decisions for his organization, which grew and grew and grew. Mario Andretti decided to stay with his strategy of building an organization that would help him win races. His strategy guided the future decisions of his organization, and he went on to become one of the greatest racecar drivers ever.

Their very different strategies led to remarkable success for both men and their organizations. Their examples provide a powerful insight into the real value of having a strategy.

DETERMINING CURRENT STRATEGY

If you develop and communicate a clear strategy for your organization, you can work together with the other members of your organization to convert that strategy into sustained success.

My approach for organizations to determine their business strategy is based on my strategy work experience with clients as well as insights from these four books: *Top Management Strategy*, *The Strategy-Focused Organization*, *Only the Paranoid Survive*, and *Blue Ocean Strategy*.[3]

The Process for Determining Your Organization's Strategy

1. Clarify your organization's current strategy.

2. Understand what has changed and what may change in your organization, in your industry, and in the marketplace.

3. Identify alternative strategies for your organization.

4. Select and communicate the strategy your organization will follow.

Clarify Your Organization's Current Strategy

I asked you to clarify your organization's current strategy in Chapter One, but I want you to give this more thought now. Clarify your organization's current strategy as much as you can by answering the questions on page 146 and 147. In doing so, you'll have a much clearer idea of what you're changing from and why you're making the change in strategy, if indeed you decide to change it.

Now try it again, completing the statements aloud in the oral version on page 148.

Practice stating your organization's current strategy aloud until you can rattle it off conversationally without looking at the written version or at any notes you have made.

Until you decide to change the strategy of your organization or profit center, use the outcome of this process to guide future decisions regarding your organization.

Here's an example of a hypothetical current strategy for a fictitious school supply business with two retail locations that serves parents with children in preschool thru eighth grade.

The Process for Clarifying Your Organization's Current Strategy (written version)

To be able to determine your organization's current strategy, complete in writing the ten statements in the strategy template below. Your answers will provide the necessary elements for describing the current strategy.

1. The financial goals we want our organization to achieve over the next three years are:

   _____

   _____

   _____.

   (You can add as much texture, detail, and complexity to your financial goals as you want.)

2. The purpose of our organization is to: _____

   _____.

   (This is why your organization exists.)

3. Primarily, we are a _____ organization.

   (Choose from customer-centric, product-centric, service-centric, price-centric, or technology-centric organization. A customer-centric company focuses on meeting a wide range of desires of a specific type of customer. A product-centric company concentrates on selling the best product in its category and continually works to improve that product. A service-centric company focuses on providing extraordinary service to customers from their initial introduction to the company's products and services through the purchasing stage and on to the maintenance phase. A price-centric company focuses on providing the product or service at the lowest price in the industry. A technology-centric company focuses on leveraging its learned body of knowledge to create value for the customer.)

4. Secondarily, we are a _____ organization.

   (Choose from customer-centric, product-centric, service-centric, price-centric, or technology-centric organization.)

5. Our customers describe our products as _____
   _____.

   (Choose from excellent, above average, average, and below average.)

6. Our customers describe our service as: _____
   _____.

   (Choose from excellent, above average, average, and below average.)

7. Our customers describe their relationship with our organization as: _____.

   (Choose from excellent, above average, average, and below average.)

8. Our customers describe the value they receive from our organization as: _____
   _____.

   (In other words, why do customers buy from your organization?)

9. The way in which we deliver value to customers is:
   _____
   _____.

   (This describes how your organization actually delivers its products and services to customers.)

10. The employees in our organization consistently behave in the following ways: _____
    _____.

    (This describes the culture in your organization.)

The Process for Clarifying Your Organization's Current Strategy (oral version)

Complete the ten statements in the strategy template below to clarify your organization's current strategy.

1. The financial goals we want our organization to achieve over the next three years are:

2. The purpose of our organization is to:

3. Primarily, our organization is:

4. Secondarily, our organization is:

5. Our customers describe our products as:

6. Our customers describe our service as:

7. Our customers describe their relationship with our organization as:

8. Our customers describe the value they receive from our organization as:

9. The way in which we deliver value to customers is:

10. The employees in our organization consistently behave in the following ways:

Case Study: Current Strategy for Pencil, Inc., a School Supply Company

Our three-year financial goals are to increase revenues by 8 percent each year while limiting expense increases to 2 percent annually. Our most important financial metric is revenue per grade. We want to diversify our revenue by making sure that no grade represents more than 15 percent of our total revenue. Right now, most of our revenue is generated by parents with students in preschool and kindergarten.

We want to expand sales with parents whose children are in grades first through eighth.

Our purpose is to be a one-stop shop for school supplies for children preschool through eighth grade. We are primarily a customer-centric business. Rather than selling the best possible product, we provide a broad array of products for students that meet the vast majority of their school needs. We are secondarily a service-centric business. If we don't have the item in our retail stores, we will order it for the customer, overnight it to their house, and not charge them for shipping.

Our customers say our products are average, our service is above average, and our relationships with them are excellent. Our customers say the value they receive from our stores is primarily in the convenience of being able to buy everything they need for school at one location. The way in which we deliver value is to have our store very organized, maintain a strong inventory, and respond to any questions our customers have as fast as we can. All of our products are organized by grade level.

Our employees are respectful and polite in interacting with one another, always show up on time, and are very good at interacting with our customers. However, they rarely disagree with one another and avoid conflict at all costs.

Notice the simplicity in this strategy. In four paragraphs, it completes all the statements laid out in the strategy template, and can be easily explained in a conversation. An effective strategy helps to guide future decisions and to clarify whether a potential activity supports it or not. The manager of this school supplies business can now decide what tactics fall within the strategy and what ones fall outside of the strategy.

Understand What Has Changed and What May Change in Your Organization, in Your Industry, and in the Marketplace

Despite being named the 1997 *Time Magazine* Man of the Year and serving as CEO and Chairman of Intel during its heyday, Andy Grove's greatest contribution to the business world may have been his explanation of what he called "strategic inflection points." In his book, *Only the Paranoid Survive: How to Exploit the Crisis Points That Challenge Every Company*, Andy Grove defined a strategic inflection point as "a time in the life of a business when its fundamentals are about to change. A strategic inflection point can be deadly when unattended to. But strategic inflection points do not always lead to disaster. When the way business is being conducted changes, it creates opportunities for players who are adept at operating in the new way."[4]

Dramatic changes can occur both inside and outside your organization. Inside your organization a dramatic change might include the development of a new product that customers buy in record numbers, the loss of a key employee to the competition, or a customer that represents 75 percent of your revenue deciding to stop doing business with you.

Outside your business a massive change might mean a competitor who develops a breakthrough product that is grabbing enormous market share overnight, a media story that suddenly places tremendous negative publicity on your business, or a gigantic change in society, such as gasoline prices tripling in eighteen months.

A dramatic change will affect your results. That's a given. What is not a given is how you respond to this "strategic inflection point." The key is to step into the details of your strategy to see what can be altered in order for your organization to flourish in the new environment it faces. When faced with a dramatic change—or even the possibility of a dramatic change—it's time to consider revamping your strategy.

Too often executives set aside a few days each fall to develop their strategy for the next year. Each year they make some adjustments to the strategy that takes their organization in a slightly different direction than the year before. There are two problems with this approach. First, you don't need to change your strategy every year. You only need to change it when faced with a dramatic change or the possibility of a dramatic change, or if your actual results are not on track with your desired results for an extended period of time. Second, sometimes you can't wait for the fall planning session. Once you realize a significant change is happening, you need to be ready to respond with possible changes to your strategy.

In auto racing, there are occasionally dramatic changes that require changes in strategy. In 1994, NASCAR held the first-ever stock car race at the Indianapolis Motor Speedway and called it the Brickyard 400. In 1994, Jeff Gordon was a third-year driver in the NASCAR Winston Cup Series. Winning the Brickyard 400 would be a major feather in his cap. However, this track was different from the other NASCAR tracks. It was designed for open-wheel racecars that go 230 mph. Winning this race would require a change in strategy for NASCAR drivers.

In her book, *One Helluva Ride: How NASCAR Swept the Nation*, Liz Clarke described how Gordon's crew chief, Ray Evernham, created a winning strategy: "Evernham researched the track as if he were writing a master's thesis, grilling Indy car veterans for their insights. He phoned Pancho Carter, who competed in seventeen Indianapolis 500s, and he spent time with four-time Indy 500 champion A. J. Foyt. He asked every question he could think of. How smooth was the surface? How did the track respond to changes in temperature? In humidity? Then he designed a special car with trick features to exploit what he had learned."[5]

When faced with a dramatic change, Evernham studied the information, identified alternatives to solve the challenges, and crafted a new strategy that allowed Jeff Gordon to win by half a second in front of 250,000 people.

In 1981, Richard Childress began a nearly twenty-year relationship with Dale Earnhardt Sr. Earnhardt, frustrated with his racing team's current owner, decided to join forces with Childress as the team owner, and the partnership went on to win the NASCAR Winston Cup six times. Keep in mind that Earnhardt won the 1980 Winston Cup and had already proved to be a terrific driver.

However, Childress realized that Earnhardt represented a dramatic change from other highly successful drivers. Instead of avoiding contact and positioning himself for a chance for victory at the end of each race, Earnhardt attacked the race from the very first minute and would bump any car in his path to get to the lead. Childress put together a strategy of combining a driver who wouldn't back off with a car that wouldn't break down.[6]

Childress allowed Earnhardt to drive for a different owner, Bud

Moore Engineering, for two years while he prepared his organization to build amazingly durable cars from the ground up. To win the NASCAR Winston Cup, the key is durability. A driver has to amass points over the course of the entire season. For Dale Earnhardt Sr. to win the Winston Cup consistently, he needed to be in incredibly durable cars. The strategy paid off and Dale Earnhardt Sr. was the Winston Cup champion in 1986, 1987, 1990, 1991, 1993, and 1994.

What dramatic change is your organization facing right now? Is there something truly significant happening inside your organization, or with your competition, or with the marketplace in general? Don't try to hide your head, avoid reality, and hope not to crash and burn. Instead be honest about what is happening around you. This honesty may lead to a strategy that will take you to accomplishments you've never dreamed of for your organization.

Identify Alternative Strategies for Your Organization

The easiest way to generate alternative strategies for consideration is to go back to The Process for Clarifying Your Organization's Current Strategy, examine each of the statements that you completed, and change your answers one at a time. After each change, step back, and consider what impact that change might have on the long-term success of your organization.

I will use my fictitious example of Pencil, Inc., the school supply business, to demonstrate how changing one statement at a time can affect the direction of the business.

Change #1: Financial Goals

Instead of striving for 8 percent annual revenue growth, a 2 percent maximum growth in expenses, and a maximum of 15 percent in revenues coming from any one grade level, say the financial goals change to 5 percent annual revenue growth, a 40 percent reduction in expenses, and no limits for revenues coming from any one grade level. How would this impact the business?

In order to reduce costs by 40 percent, the business may need to close one of its retail locations and reduce the amount of inventory in their remaining location. In order to achieve their revenue growth goals for the next three years, Pencil, Inc. may need to become more of a web-driven business where consumers could order their school supplies on line and have them delivered to their homes. Some personnel from the store reduction may end up working in the expansion of the on-line business. Free shipping would no doubt become a perk of the past—and some customer goodwill or perception of service might fall by the wayside.

Change #2: Purpose of Organization
Raison d'etre.

I just love those two words: "raison d'etre." They mean "reason for existence." You may have noticed a pattern throughout this book. Over and over, I've encouraged you to clarify your purpose: your purpose as an individual to improve personal effectiveness, your purpose as a leader for improving your influence on others, the purpose of your group in order to improve teamwork, and now the purpose of your organization in order to improve the strategic direction in which you're heading.

If you change the purpose of your organization, many aspects of its strategy would probably change as well. If Pencil, Inc. changed its purpose from "being a one-stop shop for school supplies for children preschool through eighth grade," to "enhancing the academic lives of grade-school children," the impact on its decisions could be dramatic.

Selling pencils, folders, and book bags is one thing, but improving academic performance of students is another. Pencil, Inc. might offer seminars on reading skills on-site at schools or at their locations on the weekend. They might set up a tutoring service where they connect tutors with families whose children are having academic difficulties. They might provide webinars for parents all over the country on how to get kids to embrace learning.

A shift in purpose can lead to a shift in how to deliver the value, which suppliers to work with, and what types of talent will stay in the organization and what ones will be asked to leave. Take your statement of purpose seriously, and only change it if you believe your organization will be better off over the long run. Then make sure that any ensuing decisions about your business fit within the new purpose.

Change #3: Primary Organization Type

Instead of Pencil, Inc. seeing itself as primarily a customer-centric business, what if it were primarily a technology-centric business? I explained in Chapter 1 that technology means "systemized knowledge obtained by study, observation, and experiment that is used in a practical way."

If Pencil, Inc. were primarily a technology-centric business, it might focus on leveraging knowledge about children ages four to fourteen in order to improve their academic well-being. For example, if the company learned that one hour of semiorganized games a day improved performance in the classroom, they might set up time frames at a local field for children to play soccer, baseball, and volleyball. At these games, no score would be kept by adults. The children would just have the space and equipment to play along with enough supervision to make sure no one got hurt.

Change #4: Secondary Type of Organization

Instead of secondarily being a service-centric business, what if Pencil, Inc. was secondarily a product-centric business? Their primary focus of customer-centric causes them to meet a wide array of needs for children four to fourteen years old, and this new secondary focus would mean they would focus on providing the best possible product in each way that they are trying to add value to their target audience. Consequently, they would work to have the very highest quality book bags, computers and software for children, and reading enhancement tools.

Change #5: Customers' Description of Product

Instead of the customers saying their products were average, Pencil, Inc. could make decisions so that customers thought their products were below average. If they did this, they might decide to change the emphasis of the company from being a one-stop shop to being an information business. Customers might contact them looking for information on babysitters, coaches, athletic teams, piano lessons, and so on. They might become the Google for parents of grade-school and preschool children. Their revenue source might become primarily advertising on their website and at their stores.

Change #6: Customers' Description of Service

Instead of customers saying their service was above average, Pencil, Inc. could decide to make their service so exceptional that customers routinely rated it as excellent. Instead of just mailing products overnight for free to customers when they don't have the product in the store, the company could promise to overnight all purchases greater than $50 to the customers for free. In this way, customers don't have to cart purchases home. It would also allow Pencil, Inc. to expand its website service to customers all over the country, and possibly the world.

Change #7: Customers' Relationship with Organization

Rather than customers describing their relationship with Pencil, Inc. as excellent, what if they described it as average? In other words, customers would come into the stores, and no one would greet them or ask them what they were looking for or what problems they wanted resolved. Instead there would be a minimum number of employees in the store. In this scenario, the company might slash costs and pass along the savings to the customer.

Change #8: Customers' Description of Value Received

Instead of Pencil, Inc. having customers say the value they receive from their stores is primarily in the convenience of being able to buy everything they need for school at one location, what if they worked to have customers say the primary value they received was great academic counseling that led to improved preparation for high school?

When you change the desired value for customers, you also begin to change your brand. If Pencil, Inc. wants to become known for excellent academic counseling, it needs to change its advertising and personnel.

Change #9: The Way Value Is Delivered to Customers

Pencil, Inc. wants to be known as a one-stop shopping experience for children's school supplies, and the way they want to deliver value is to have their stores very organized and have their employees respond to any questions the customers ask as fast as they can. What if they changed the way they created a one-stop shopping experience?

Instead of having an organized store and answering questions for customers as they walked around the store, what if they had customers go on line from their home computer to see all the products they had to offer? A customer could just click on any item he or she wanted to purchase along with the amount of that item.

Back at the store, an employee could go and assemble all of those products into bags and have the entire purchase ready for the customer to pick up later in the day. In this way, the customer would still have a one-stop shopping experience, but wouldn't have to walk the aisles looking for items.

Change #10: Employee Behavior

Pencil, Inc. currently has employees who are respectful and polite in interacting with one another, always show up on time, and are very good at interacting with the customers. They also rarely disagree with one another and avoid conflict at all costs. While this culture creates a very pleasant environment for employees and customers, it may not lead to breakthrough innovations.

What if the business decided to create a culture that encouraged healthy debates where employees could challenge each other to find better ways to add value to customers? Even though this atmosphere could be more stressful in the short term, it could also be much more invigorating for employees over the long term. From these discussions, great ideas could emerge that might improve the business significantly.

The reason I went through all ten parts of the strategy template was to demonstrate that a single change in any part of your strategy can result in a completely new approach to generate sustainable, profitable growth. In other words, one change can lead to a whole new business strategy, which might be more successful than anything that's ever been done in that industry.

I suggest you take the Pencil, Inc. case study and go through each of the ten statements in the strategy template, make one change at a time that is different than the one I suggested, and try to envision what change that might have on the business. This is a good exercise for the bigger exercise that lies ahead of you.

Then, and more importantly, I suggest you work with the top eight to twelve members of your organization and go through the first three steps in the process for determining the best strategy for your organization. Remember to embrace simplicity and avoid process creep. In summary, here are the first three steps.

The first step is to fill in the strategy template. The second step is to identify what dramatic changes have occurred or likely will occur inside or outside of your organization. The third step is to go through each of your responses and change them one at a time in order to generate alternative strategies for your organization.

Select and Communicate the Strategy Your Organization Will Follow

When you've gone through the first three steps, you are now at decision time. Notice I didn't say further research time. After you understand your current strategy, the dramatic changes that have occurred or will likely occur, and the strategic alternatives you have in front of you, you need to make a decision.

Now you have a choice: either stick with the strategy you currently have in place or change the strategy to something new. If you decide to remain with your current strategy, then communicate that decision clearly to the people in your organization and let them know why you've decided to stay with that strategy.

If you select a new strategy, then carefully complete the statements again in the process for clarifying your organization's current strategy. This way, you and every other member of your organization know exactly what the new strategy is and can use it in making future decisions about the organization. Then communicate the new strategy as clearly and as often as you can in a wide variety of settings for all the members of your organization.

Strategies either sit on a shelf, or they get communicated. The former die and the latter come to life. Don't let your organization lose the Management 500 because you let yours die on the shelf.

There is no perfect strategy. There are only relatively good strategies and relatively bad strategies. A relatively good strategy is one that converts a dramatic change into a solid opportunity for your business, and intentionally intersects the values, strengths, and passions of the people in your organization with the desired outcomes for your business and your customers.

Select the strategy you believe gives your organization the best opportunity to generate sustainable, profitable growth over the next three years, and then let everyone in your organization know that this is the strategy going forward.

FACTORS THAT INFLUENCE THE SUCCESS OF A STRATEGY

Having a strategy, even a really good one, is meaningless unless you use the strategy to guide decisions that actually produce better results. You've only been successful when the results have been produced, not when the strategy gets explained to your employees. Here are four keys to convert a strategy into success.

A True Opportunity

Is your strategy focused on an opportunity that really matters to your customers and potential customers? When Apple came out with the iPhone, they clearly hit a home run. The iPhone fit within Apple's Digital Hub strategy and clearly took advantage of the massive cell phone market. That was a great opportunity in the marketplace that also fit within their strategy.

Leander Kahney, in his book *Inside Steve's Brain*, wrote, "The digital hub strategy is possibly the most important thing Jobs has laid out in a keynote speech. It shows how adherence to a simple, well-articulated idea can successfully guide corporate strategy, and influence everything from the development of products to the layout of retail stores."[7]

Jobs's concept was that the computer was the hub of the digital lifestyle and many of the digital devices that made up that lifestyle. He felt that the computer enhanced the digital devices, and that Apple could enhance both the computer and the digital devices, thus improving the digital lifestyle of consumers. This simple articulation of the Apple strategy in 2001 led to the creation of the iPod and iPhone.

What opportunity in the marketplace does your strategy focus on? What dramatic change has occurred in your company, in your industry, or in the overall market that you can convert to your advantage that will really matter to customers? Before you invest too much time, energy, and money into your strategy be sure it matters to people who will pay you.

Clarity

Even though the strategy template asks you to complete the statements in writing, I believe you are best served by making your strategy statement conversational. First, take the time to think through your answers and write them down. Then practice saying the answers aloud, over and over again, until you can say them without looking at the paper. Finally, explain your organization's strategy in a variety of conversations (start with your family and friends) until it comes out smoothly.

When you can explain the strategy in a normal conversation, you have reached a point where it is ready to be rolled out to the rest of the organization. People can deal with incredible changes in their lives, but dealing with the unknown is very hard to do. It causes anxiety and stress. If your organization is moving to a new strategy, one key to success is for the members of the organization to understand clearly what it is that describes their organization and guides the future decisions about the organization.

Organizational Support

A great strategy has no chance of success if no one in your organization supports it. The best way that I know to gain support for a strategy is to get a variety of people involved in the development of the strategy. I'm talking about collaborating in the strategy formulation process, but I'm not talking about forming a democracy where majority rules. I encourage you to give a copy of the blank version of The Process for Clarifying Your Organization's Strategy to your top eight to twelve executives. Ask them to fill it out and be prepared to discuss their completed statements in an open collaborative conversation with all of you in a room.

Let the group know at the beginning that you want to have healthy debates over the ideas, you want people to look for ways to combine ideas to develop even better ideas, and you want people to be open to seeing how one idea may lead to a completely different idea that is even better.

However, also make it clear that in the end you will make the final decisions on what the organization's strategy will look like. You cannot compromise your way to a great strategy where each person gets a say on a little piece of the strategy. That leads to a very weak strategy. As the manager of a business—or of a part of one—one of your most important responsibilities is to establish the final strategy. By using a collaborative process, you can make it very clear that you listen to your employees, consider their input, and are willing to explain how you came to the final decision that you selected.

Patience

If you want a strategy to be successful, then you have to be patient. A strategy is not an accomplishment. It guides decisions that ultimately lead to accomplishments. Those accomplishments take time to occur. You do need milestones to give you some indication as to whether or not your organization is moving in the right direction, but you have to remain patient.

In September 1999, Jeff Gordon's crew chief, Ray Evernham, resigned and his entire over-the-wall crew quit at the end of the 1999 season. Gordon, Evernham, and most of this group had won the NASCAR Winston Cup in 1995, 1996, and 1997. In 1999, Gordon became the youngest driver in history to win the most races in a season five years in a row.

Beginning in 2000, Gordon worked with a new crew chief, Robbie Loomis, and a whole new over-the-wall crew. Slowly but steadily

Loomis, Gordon, and Brian Whitesell, the new team manager, developed a strategy for winning the Winston Cup. However, the results did not roll in right away.

Gordon described how he felt in early 2000 after a particularly disappointing performance, "I understood that this was a process, and it would, indeed, take time to rebuild. I also knew that Robbie and this new team needed to see me and hear my assurances. It wasn't enough for me to chat with the crew chief and go my own way. I had to play a larger role. I had to face the realities of my new position. This was where I had to jump in and make a difference."[8]

Jeff Gordon and his team did remain patient with their strategy and with each other and went on to win the NASCAR Winston Cup in 2001. They also led the Winston series in number of races won, poles won, and top finishes.

Do you believe in your strategy enough to remain patient with it over the next three years? Or are you going to jump to a new strategy the first quarter that you don't hit your projected numbers? Sustainable, profitable growth can come from patiently adhering to a good strategy and executing the details of the plan that support the strategy. You won't achieve sustainable success if you change what is guiding your organization every six months.

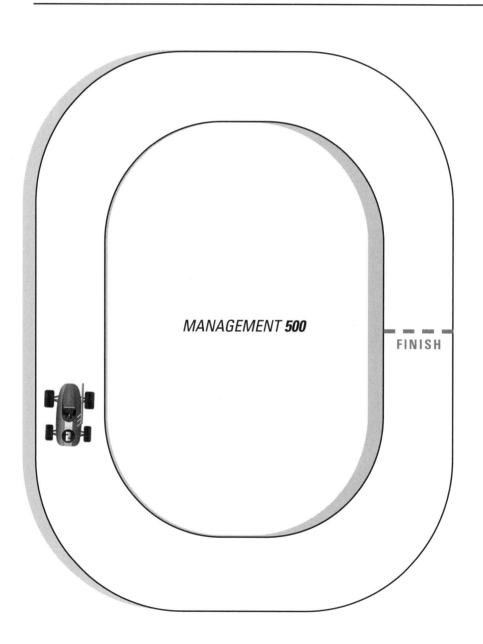

CHAPTER NINE

MANAGEMENT *500*

FINISH

SPEED UP
BRAND EQUITY

The world of professional auto racing is a world of building brand equity. In auto racing there are two goals: win races and build brands. Strong brands in the auto racing universe attract sponsors, endorsements, and car buyers. The stronger the brand, the more success everyone experiences. This is true for the drivers, the car manufacturer, and the racing teams.

I asked Geoff Smith, president of Roush Fenway Racing, which is sponsored in part by Ford Motor Corporation, how winning in NASCAR helps to build the Ford brand, grow sales of Ford cars for consumers, and strengthen the brands of their other sponsors. He said:

> Winning helps all sponsors, including Ford, in a number of fundamental ways. First, winning generates a plethora of "free" exposure of the sponsors' brands through print media, digital media, print advertising that other sharing sponsors buy, promotions that other sponsors buy, and so forth (i.e., a cross-promotion benefit without having to pay).
>
> Second, winning helps create and confirm that each brand is a performance brand, that each company is competitive, and that being better than the competition is an important brand value that is being reinforced.
>
> Third, winning delivers more fan market share to that team and

its sponsors. While fans understand that they must support sponsors with purchases of their products and services in order to have their favorite team find and retain sponsorship, winning creates disproportionate attention of the fans to those brands.

Fourth, in the case of Ford, there is an underlying connection between the quality of the race cars and the quality of the production cars. The better one performs, the more likely it is people will believe the production cars and trucks will be better than the competition.

Fifth, most of our sponsors are number one or number two in worldwide sales for their category of business. That means virtually all of their employees view themselves as being successful and competitive. Performance on the race track acts as an icon to confirm those values. The more success on the track, the more interest the employees have to support the program and insure that it is activated properly and with full support internally.[1]

Ed Laukes, Corporate Manager of Toyota Motorsports Marketing and Operations, is the executive at Toyota who oversees all of the company's motor sports activities in the United States. If it involves Toyota and racing, then Ed is involved in some way. I asked him how Toyota's success in NASCAR helps to strengthen the Toyota brand for consumers with its cars, trucks, SUVs, and other products.

He said, "NASCAR is part of the mainstream in America and that is our ultimate goal at Toyota. We use a variety of ways to strengthen our brand and our involvement with NASCAR is one of them. Success in NASCAR connects with potential customers as well as our current consumer base and the general racing fans in the United States, particularly in the midwestern, southeastern, and southern regions."

I then asked Ed what he felt the keys are for any company, regardless of its size or industry, to build a strong brand.

He said,

First, identify exactly what you want to accomplish. Then always be true to who you say you are. For example, at Toyota we want to be the most respected car company in the world. The key for us is to always be loyal to our dealers, associates and consumers no matter what the circumstances. The secret is to maintain credibility in the marketplace and never deviate.

For example, we've been working with the Mars family. They are true to what they say they are. They want to provide a quality product at a reasonable price that consumers enjoy eating. They've stayed true to who they are for over a hundred years. Decide who you want to be. When you wake up 100 years from now, what do you want people to say about your company? Then stay true to your beliefs and values in every decision you make.

Then I asked Ed how Toyota Motorsports builds effective teamwork considering Toyota works with multiple vehicles, racing teams, and racing series.

He said, "We treat everyone the same way. We look at a race team the same way we look at all of our dealers. We gather a lot of information that we share with everyone. We want every race team we work with to succeed. I spend more of my time and energy on what we call the 'rookie teams' trying to help them succeed than on our more experienced teams. Our belief is we haven't succeeded until each of our teams has won at least one race."

Toyota joined the NASCAR Sprint Cup Series in 2007 and by 2008 they were achieving extraordinary success, particularly with the Joe Gibbs Racing (JGR) Team, which had Kyle Busch, Tony Stewart, and Denny Hamlin as their drivers. I asked Ed how Toyota was able to achieve success so quickly. He responded by saying:

> We had been in the truck series for a few years, and from that experience we learned a lot about the people and the processes involved in NASCAR. That was valuable information when we entered the Sprint Cup Series.
>
> However, the biggest key to our initial success was partnering with the Gibbs family and the Joe Gibbs Racing organization. The combination of the long-term, experienced core of people at JGR, coupled with the great power plant and engineering support from TRD, U.S.A. (Toyota Racing Development) really turned out to be the key to our rapid success in the Sprint Cup Series. The nucleus of people at Joe Gibbs Racing is so strong and their turnover is so

low that they brought the capability to win right away. When you combine that level of skill and experience with the level of expertise we have at TRD and three extraordinary drivers, you have a very powerful team.

Finally, I asked Ed how he provides leadership to such a diverse organization, and he answered:

> I try to lead by example. The key to being an effective leader is to stay true to the reality of who you are and what you expect. Always be honest. That has always worked in my professional career. People may not agree with you, but they appreciate that they are always going to hear the truth.
>
> When dealing with independent business people, they have to trust you in order for you to succeed as a leader. So you have to deal with them honestly. If you are true to who you are, they will respect you as a leader. It's the same as in building a brand. If you stay true to yourself and never deviate, then people will trust and know they can count on you.[2]

When the Ferrari Formula 1 Racing Team wins a Formula 1 Grand Prix World Championship, money from sponsors goes up and Ferrari sales around the world improve. The key to the Ferrari brand is sustained winning. However, from 1979 to 1995, Ferrari did not win a Formula 1 world championship. That was hurting their brand.

After Michael Schumacher won the Formula 1 Grand Prix World Championship for Benetton in 1994 and 1995, Ferrari offered him $25 million a year to be one of their two drivers. That's how important winning is to a brand. Schumacher joined the team, and the rest is history.[3] He went on to win the world championship for Ferrari every year from 2000–2004.

If a person feels he or she has to overcome the odds and persevere through difficulties to achieve success, then Dale Earnhardt Sr. is a pretty darn good role model. Earnhardt Sr. is one of the greatest examples of an everyman who persevered until he succeeded. Perhaps the greatest individual brand in NASCAR history, Earnhardt Sr. was seen as just an ordinary guy who could be your good buddy and still win the Winston Cup every year. By 2000, twenty years after he won his first Winston Cup with virtually no money in his pocket, *Forbes* ranked him fortieth on the list of its 100 Richest Celebrities with his annual income estimated at $24.5 million.[4]

In his first few years as a NASCAR driver, Jeff Gordon was known as "Wonderboy," at least that's what Dale Earnhardt Sr. called him. Combining his good looks and amazing winning percentage at a young age, he became wildly popular among NASCAR fans, particularly female fans. Not only did his winnings go up from racing, but his endorsement earnings grew even faster. Within five years of being a NASCAR driver, Gordon was signed by William Morris, the world's largest talent agency.[5]

NASCAR itself has created incredible brand equity since the day it was founded on December 14, 1947, by Bill France Sr. It held its first race in 1948 and named its first annual champion in 1949. In the early days NASCAR was very small and no one made very much money. Over the past sixty-plus years, the France family, which has owned NASCAR from day one, has steadily built the NASCAR brand into a multibillion-dollar enterprise that owns multiple racing series, numerous race tracks, licensing of NASCAR-related products, and much more.[6]

The actual races are another aspect of great branding. Races like the Daytona 500 are amazing events that draw incredible crowds. Of course, the largest sporting event in the world in terms of attendance is a professional auto race: the Indianapolis 500, which draws in excess of 250,000 people every year; the first Indianapolis 500 was held in 1911.

Winning the race adds tremendous brand equity to the winning driver and racing team. However, it's costly to earn that brand. In 2004, "one driver in one car for one month cost about 1 million to 1.5 million dollars."[7] Building a great brand requires effort, money, courage, and, most importantly, great performance.

Of course, people who drive street cars watch people who drive racecars. And those customers love to be associated with their favorite drivers and cars. When a favorite driver wins in a Chevrolet, Ferrari, Ford, Pontiac, Toyota, Buick, Dodge, BMW, or Plymouth, the impact on the brand and the car sales is incredible. The same is true if the racecar owner also owns a car dealership such as Rick Hendrick, who owns multiple Chevrolet car dealerships and Hendrick Motorsports, which has won several championships in NASCAR.

Dale Earnhardt Sr. and Jeff Gordon sold a lot of Chevrolets by winning the NASCAR Winston Cup eleven times while driving Chevrolets. The ironic thing is a NASCAR stock car bears little resemblance to a street car once you get under the hood, but that doesn't hurt sales. It's about being associated with a great brand, and that is what drives car sales. Not just racecar-branded sales, but all car sales. Customers want to be associated with a great brand. Lessons on how to build a great brand come from cars for consumers as much as from racing cars.

BMW is known as "the ultimate driving machine." That brand is incredibly strong, and is reinforced year after year when BMW is consistently named the best sports sedan in the world by *Car and Driver* magazine.[8] However, Toyota, with a completely different brand than BMW, is one of the world's largest automakers.

There are powerful lessons on branding that can be drawn from racing teams and car manufacturers. In order to uncover those lessons, let's start with a few key questions:

1. What is brand equity and why is it important?

2. How do you build brand equity in any industry?

3. How do you damage brand equity?

Let's take a look at each of these questions.

WHAT IS BRAND EQUITY AND WHY IS IT IMPORTANT?

A brand is the perception of value that a potential buyer has of a specific organization's products and services. An organization can be represented by the name of a single person or the name of the entire company. Tiger Woods has a brand, Jeff Gordon has a brand, NASCAR has a brand, GE has a brand, and your company has a brand. Consequently, brand equity is the collective value that potential buyers associate with a given organization's products and services.

If 100 potential buyers are willing to exchange on average $1,000 for Company A's products and services, then the organization has a brand equity of $100,000. If the perceived value of that organization's products and services goes up and the number of people willing to buy that value expands, then the brand equity goes up. For example, say the number of people willing to buy Company A's products and services goes up to 200 people and the amount they are willing to exchange for that organization's products and services on average goes up to $2,000. In that case, the brand equity is $400,000.

While every organization has brand equity, in some cases that brand equity is almost zero. Take the television show, *American Idol*. Twenty-four singers make it on TV, and then each week singers are eliminated until finally there is only one person left. The brand equity of most of the singers when they get on the show is virtually zero. Very few buyers of music CDs would buy these singers' CDs before that season's *American Idol* starts.

However, as the weeks pass by, the individuals become better known, the perceived value of their music goes up, and their brand equity increases. In some cases, after having been on *American Idol*, these individuals go on to sell a lot of albums, get movie contracts, and appear on Broadway. These are the same people with the same talents they had before they were on the show, but suddenly their brand equity has increased.

Why?

Notice that just being on the show did not increase their brand equity. They had to have developed their craft as singers and performers before audience members attached perceived value to them. On the other hand, just having developed their craft as singers was not enough to increase their brand equity. Buyers actually had to perceive them as being valuable. They had to have the ability to deliver value and the perception on the part of potential buyers that they could deliver value.

Dale Earnhardt Sr. was a very good racecar driver in 1978, and he was broke. In 1980, after he won the NASCAR Winston Cup, he was a very good driver and he was quickly becoming very wealthy. He suddenly had sponsors like Wrangler Jeans that he had never had before. His brand equity was on the rise, and more and more sponsors and fans liked the value they perceived receiving from him.[9]

Brand equity requires both the delivery of value and the perception on the part of buyers that value is being delivered. In order to strengthen your organization's brand equity you have to continually increase the value your organization delivers to buyers and continually improve the perception of the value you deliver. One without the other is insufficient for increasing brand equity.

If your organization only improves the marketing of the value it delivers or if it only increases the value it can deliver without letting anyone know that it can deliver more value, it won't consistently improve its brand equity. Without stronger brand equity, you essentially start the next year from the same spot you started the last year. You can't win the Management 500 and achieve three consecutive years of significant, profitable growth unless you continually strengthen your organization's brand equity.

Imagine a singer leaves *American Idol* with much stronger brand equity than he or she started with and sells 50,000 CDs. If that person doesn't improve his or her ability to deliver musical value to buyers and doesn't become known by more people as a deliverer of musical value, then the person will sell 50,000 or fewer copies of their second CD. On the other hand, if the person improves his or her ability as a singer and other buyers find out about the value in the first CD, then that person's brand equity goes up and their sales of subsequent CDs will go up.

Imagine your organization generated $11 million in sales this year. If your organization doesn't either improve the value it can deliver to customers or let other customers know the value it can deliver, then it will make at most $11 million next year. If that happens, then you've lost the Management 500. Building brand equity is essential to consistently improving the profitable growth of your business.

HOW DO YOU BUILD BRAND EQUITY IN ANY INDUSTRY?

Having worked as a consultant with great brands like Toyota, McDonald's, Marriott, Coca-Cola, and Boeing over the past eleven years, I've learned a lot about what to do and what not to do in order to build brand equity. As you go through these seven steps, I encourage you not only to embrace simplicity, but to also maintain the courage and discipline not to go on wild tangents in the pursuit of a stronger brand.

The Process for Speeding Up Brand Equity

1. Define the customer value category you want to own.

2. Provide excellent quality.

3. Consistently let buyers and connectors know the value your organization delivers.

4. Maintain authenticity.

5. Patiently persevere.

6. Continually improve the value you deliver.

7. Win.

Define the Customer Value Category You Want to Own

My favorite book on building brand equity is *Positioning: The Battle for Your Mind* by Al Ries and Jack Trout.[10] What I learned from *Positioning* is that every person holds in his or her mind a ranking of specific products and services for every type of value they want to purchase.

For example, if you say, "family vacation destination," each consumer will have a ranking of their top choices. The main point of the book is if you're in the business of selling a family vacation destination, the only ranking you really want is the top ranking in the minds of potential buyers. The only other possible ranking worth having is second place because then you may be able to be the alternative brand to the top choice.

Other than that, you're out of luck for that customer value category. You might as well shut the organization down because you're going to experience years of utter frustration where no matter how hard you work you can't consistently generate significant, profitable growth. Customers go for number one most of the time, number two some of the time, and numbers three through ten just occasionally.

However, and this is the exciting part, you get to define the customer value category you're in. Rather than competing in a head-to-head competition with whoever is number one, what if you defined your customer value category as "family vacation destination within ninety miles of Chicago?" Now you've eliminated a whole bunch of competitors.

Within that new category, your goal is to be number one in the minds of potential buyers or at the very least to be number two. If you're number three or worse, then you have to compete on something else, price for example. If you do that, then you need to craft a new customer value category: best family vacation destination within ninety miles of Chicago for under $300.

You're not stuck forever in one customer value category. By crystallizing the customer value category you're competing in, you can narrow your focus to deliver a performance that will put you at number one or number two in that category. Over time you can redefine the customer value category you want to compete in.

When Walt Disney started in Hollywood in 1923, he felt he couldn't possibly compete in the world of full-length films. Instead he narrowed his customer value category to "animated short films shown before full-length films." In doing so, he was able to quickly position his company as number one in that category and build a reputation for delivering excellent value through the success of short films like *Silly Symphonies* and *Three Little Pigs*. Then he focused on redefining his customer value category into "full-length animated films." Neal Gabler, in his book, *Walt Disney*, describes it this way:

> In mid-1933, at the very time he was enjoying the enormous success of *Three Little Pigs*, he decided that he needed to chart a new course for the studio—something big and dramatic. For years he had suffered from the vagaries of the business of producing shorts and from the relatively meager profits they delivered.
>
> Though the *Silly Symphonies* fetched rentals that were 50 percent

higher than those of competitors' cartoons, they also cost appreciably more to make. Walt wrote in 1941 "We sensed we had gone about as far as we could in the short subject field without getting ourselves into a rut. We needed this new adventure to jar loose some new enthusiasm and inspiration."[11]

That new adventure was to create the first full-length animated film, *Snow White and the Seven Dwarfs*. In doing so, Walt Disney created an entirely new customer value category to operate within. In later years, he catapulted his organization's profits once again when he created the "theme park" category with the making of Disneyland.

The first step to build a brand is to define the customer value category you want to operate within. Define it as clearly as you can. How would you describe the customer value that you can realistically become the best in the world at providing? That's an important question. Take your time and work with the top members of your organization to define the customer value category in which you can be ranked by potential buyers as number one or number two in the world.

Don't be intimidated by "in the world," because the world of potential buyers for what your organization has to offer is whatever you define it to be. For example, if your organization sells accounting services, you could define the customer value category in any of the following ways:

- Best accounting services in St. Louis.

- Best accounting services in the Midwest.

- Best accounting services for under $100 in the United States.

- Best accounting services for entrepreneurs with fewer than five employees.

As you decide on the customer value category you want to compete in just make sure your organization can be preferably number one or at least number two in that category. Otherwise, your organization will never become known as a great place for delivering value.

Provide Excellent Quality

The next step to building brand equity is to deliver excellent quality. The quality you provide to customers is the value they receive from the performance of your products and services. While every business is in the quality business, what constitutes quality varies from company to company because quality is dependent on what matters to that company's customers. Once you know the customer value category you want to operate in, the next key is to provide excellent quality within that category. Potential buyers have far too many options to settle for anything less than excellent quality.

Quality refers to the number of mistakes per million parts in a manufacturing process. It also refers to the refreshing taste of a dessert at a frozen custard stand and the speed with which a pizza is delivered and the friendliness of a hostess at a local restaurant. Your marketing theme will soon be ridiculed if the actual performance doesn't live up to the promises made.

A great brand attracts and keeps lots and lots of great customers, but you can't advertise what doesn't exist. If you're going to tell potential buyers that they will receive a specific type of performance, then your organization has to deliver that level of quality. That's known as the brand promise. If you break that promise, customers won't trust you again in the future.

Then the challenge becomes to constantly enhance the quality you deliver. Quality is a dynamic entity. You never check it off your to-do list. You improve it every day, or you fall backward. The same method for enhancing quality can be used no matter what business you are in. Here are five steps to improve quality.

1. *Know what performance customers are looking for from you.* Do your customers desire you to deliver faster (FedEx), break down less often (Toyota), provide a great driving experience (BMW), make the purchasing process easier (amazon.com), deliver breakthrough ideas (IDEO), or deliver fast, accurate, and friendly service (McDonald's)? Don't be married to a certain product, service, or profit margin. Focus on the performance you are expected to deliver.

2. *Identify your current standard of performance.* How are you really performing in the areas that customers expect you to perform in? Go ask your

customers this question: "In terms of our performance for you, what are we doing really well, what are we average or below average at doing compared to what you want, and how could we perform better for you?" If you ask fifteen customers this question, you will start to get an idea of your current reality.

Then shop the competition. Study the performance they deliver. Look at it from the customer's point of view. Even a subtle idea like having a greeter in a quick-service restaurant can be a difference maker. What is the competition doing better than you right now?

3. *Focus on only two points.* As you work to enhance quality, focus only on the point just ahead of the best performer in the world and the point just ahead of where you are right now. Who is the best performer in the world in your particular area of performance? What makes that organization's performance better than yours? That is the only point that matters to customers. They want to be with the best of the best.

While keeping the highest standard in the world in mind, focus your efforts on getting to the point just ahead of where you are right now. Each day move forward at least one step in terms of providing greater quality. Keep moving forward even when you pass the spot just ahead of the best performer in the world.

4. *Be aware of the Tiger Woods syndrome.* There is one danger to be on the lookout for. One day *you* will be the best in the world in your particular performance area. Then what do you do? Tiger Woods and Michael Jordan faced that problem, but instead of looking back at the second best performer they kept their eyes focused on raising their own performance bar. If you are the best performer in the world at what you do, ask yourself one simple question, "How can I perform better tomorrow in the areas that matter the most to my customers?"

5. *Loop back with customers.* Customers have a neat way of keeping companies grounded in reality. Just in case you thought about coasting on past performances, remember that customers don't care about past performances. A great past performance may bring them back again, but the performance they are looking for from you right now is the performance you are delivering at the moment, not the one you gave yesterday. Continue to engage customers in meaningful conversations about the quality they receive from you each day and find out what would make it better.

Brand equity increases as quality rises. Every time you increase your relevant performance for customers, it's like putting money in the bank. Customers become more loyal, they purchase more of your products and services, they tell other people about the quality you offer, and they keep coming back for years and years. Excellent quality is a key part of what fuels victory in the Management 500.

Consistently Let Buyers and Connectors Know the Value Your Organization Delivers

My second favorite book on branding is *The Tipping Point: How Little Things Can Make a Big Difference* by Malcolm Gladwell. He wrote, "Ideas and products and messages and behaviors spread just like viruses do." He then explained that there are three characteristics of an epidemic: contagious behavior, little changes having a big effect, and changes happening in one big moment rather than occurring gradually over time.[12]

Leaps in brand equity occur in the same way. Even though the brand, or the organization behind the brand, has usually been in place for a long time, the quantum leap in brand equity takes place over a short period of time. A few key people get excited about the brand and suddenly it catches on like wildfire. It happens for big businesses and small businesses.

The keys are to understand the dynamics that generate extraordinary growth in brand equity and to have your organization ready when the moment occurs. In other words, you have to have a strong foundation in place to handle success, but you also have to help generate that growth. NASCAR was around for a long time before its brand equity exploded. Google was around for a very short time before its brand equity took off. The Walt Disney Company's brand equity didn't really speed up until 1955, nearly thirty years after the company was formed, with the opening of the Disneyland theme park.

One of Gladwell's main points is that the few key people who dramatically affect the spreading of an idea, product, or service to other people are the connectors, salespeople, and experts.[13] In my words, connectors are people who introduce individuals or groups of people to each other. Salespeople are the ones who sell other people on the value of the idea, product, or service. Experts are those people who know more than most anyone else about the idea, product, or service.

Let's say you sell a special type of bicycle via the Internet. Tom is a customer of yours, loves your bike, and loves talking about your bike. Sue is a connector. She knows Tom and a whole bunch of other people and likes to introduce people to each other. If you want to spread the idea of buying your bike, then Tom is important to you and so is Sue. Tom will sell the idea of buying your bike to Sue's friends. This will just happen naturally in the normal flow of conversations.

However, there's one more person who's important: Mary, the person who is the expert on the bicycle industry. Tom's enthusiasm for your bike may get other people excited about going to your website, but only Mary's expertise will convince people that it's worth the investment you're asking for.

If you want your brand equity to grow rapidly, you need the Toms, Sues, and Marys of the world. Here's the necessary sequence to grow brand equity: provide excellent quality in a clear customer value category, gain customers who will rave to their friends and colleagues about the value they received from your products and services, and have industry experts who can vouch for the credibility of your products and services. The more you can simplify this flow of events and get them to happen faster and more often, the quicker your brand equity will grow.

In order to get salespeople, connectors, and experts to talk about your products and services the key is to inject value into the marketplace for both customers and potential customers. As people experience the value your organization has to offer, assuming that it is excellent value, the more likely they are to talk about it.

During the time when Nintendo's Wii interactive video games first started coming on the market, my family was at a shopping mall. We saw the display for Wii baseball, tennis, soccer, and bowling. Each of us got to play the games for free. We had a great time as a family. Soon the Wii made it onto Santa's Christmas Wish List for our family. After we received it we thoroughly enjoyed it and told our families and friends all about it.

What can your organization do to inject more of the value it has to offer into the marketplace so customers and potential customers can experience it? Can you give a free sample of the value that you have to offer? Can you provide additional value for a thirty- to sixty-day time period for good customers so they can see what they are missing?

Effective advertising will help you attract some customers, but it won't help you rapidly build brand equity. That comes about from enthused customers talking to other people they meet about your products and services, and industry experts establishing the credibility of your products and services for those potential customers.

Maintain Authenticity

What really has been the secret to BMW's success over the past fifty years? David Kiley, author of *Driven: Inside BMW, the Most Admired Car Company in the World*, wrote, "The smarter strategy, but one that is harder to execute, is to establish brand identity and to have that identity anchor, color, and permeate all the products and processes so the brand and products are mutually dependent, growing in lockstep. This is what BMW has done better than any other car company over the decades and better than most companies outside the auto industry as well."[14]

With its branding statement of "The Ultimate Driving Machine" guiding its every decision, BMW has built a reputation for being authentic, which means its brand is both genuine and consistent. "Auto industry historian Martin Buckley says, 'As the marquee developed in later years, this learned behavior seemed to become instinctive. BMW always felt and looked right, always had a distinctiveness, and always seemed to find customers happy to pay high prices for its product. This was not an achievement of engineering, but of management and organization.'"[15]

A non-genuine brand is created when an organization mimics every move that the best company in that industry makes. If the best company raises prices, so does the non-genuine company. If the best company comes out with a great new innovative product, the non-genuine company tries to replicate it. Non-genuine brands rarely build substantial brand equity because they are seen as me-too companies.

A genuine brand leverages the actual values, strengths, and passions that exist inside the organization to deliver value that customers really want. It doesn't take long for customers to determine a fake brand in the making, but they remember the genuine brands for a long time. You don't have to worry about BMW moving away from its brand promise of focusing on the joy of driving a high-performance automobile.

In order to build brand equity, you need to make sure that you build an authentic brand where your products and services are genuine and consistent over time. Each year for ten straight years, I did multiple projects for both Marriott International and McDonald's Corporation, which are two of the greatest and most authentic brands in the world.

Marriott's brand is based on friendly service. During those ten years, I spent countless hours behind the scenes with Marriott employees. This was during their heyday at the end of the twentieth century, during the nightmare period surrounding September 11, 2001, and during their great years in 2004–2008. Through it all, I saw the Marriott employees treat each other with friendliness and respect. In that way, I knew they were being authentic in the ways they interacted with the public.

McDonald's brand is based on quality food, fast and accurate and friendly service, clean bathrooms and restaurants and parking lots, and a good value for the price. When customers go to McDonald's they expect a down-to-earth eating experience with no frills but lots of smiles and employees who are eager to serve them.

Over the eleven years I worked with McDonald's, I met somewhere in the neighborhood of 400 McDonald's corporate executives and managers and 400 McDonald's owner/operators. Out of those 800 people, I can only remember three who were not friendly, down-to-earth, and hardworking individuals. These rare individuals, who spent more time arguing management theories than discussing real customer issues, ultimately were asked to leave McDonald's.

Of the other 797 people, several started as crew members when they were sixteen years old. However, they never lost their commitment to staying down-to-earth and genuine for their employees and customers. The McDonald's brand that is on display every day at McDonald's restaurants all over the world is incredibly successful because it is incredibly authentic.

Is your brand authentic? Does your brand bubble up in a genuine manner from the values, strengths, and passions in your organization, or is it just a copy of some other successful brand? Is your brand consistent, or does it change what it stands for every couple of years? In order to build brand equity, you need an authentic brand that is consistent and genuine.

Patiently Persevere

In 1986, Steve Jobs bought Pixar, the computer-generated imagery company, from LucasFilms. Nine, I repeat *nine*, years later Pixar came out with its first full-length computer-animated film, *Toy Story*. However, when they hit the ground running, they were going full speed ahead. The first nine films Pixar created (*Toy Story*, *A Bug's Life*, *Toy Story 2*, *Monsters, Inc.*, *Finding Nemo*, *The Incredibles*, *Cars*, *Ratatouille*, and *Wall-E*) made it to #1 at the box office. I bet the tenth will as well.

Nine years. Do you have the patience to steadily build your brand until it becomes number one or number two in the customer value category you've selected?

Jeff Gordon drove in more than 600 races in his lifetime before he won his first Winston Cup. Bobby Unser drove for fifteen years before he even qualified to race in the Indianapolis 500. Dale Earnhardt Sr. worked in his father's garage and struggled for more than ten years to even get a racecar until he made it at NASCAR in 1979.

Do you have the patience to invest ten years or more of your organization's life into building incredible brand equity? If not, you very well may not create a brand that produces sustainable, profitable growth for the long term. And here's the really hard part. You don't know when your brand equity is suddenly going to speed ahead. This requires maintaining a firm belief in future success while not knowing when that future success is going to happen. I know it's hard, and that's why building an incredible brand rarely happens in any industry.

Continually Improve the Value You Deliver

To me, Toyota is one of the most commonsense companies in the world. I can sum up their entire approach to business with two words: get better. I first interacted with Toyota when I was the keynote speaker at the 2006 Toyota Financial Services National Sales Conference. In preparation for that speech, I read books about Toyota, I studied the orientation program they gave for new employees, and, most important, I traveled to four different cities in the United States to meet the folks who work for Toyota Financial Services.

I sat in several of their training sessions, visited Toyota and Lexus dealerships, and had the opportunity to talk with about twenty-five TFS executives and managers and six dealer principals. As I talked with these individuals one word kept coming up: "kaizen." Before I met anyone at Toyota, I knew the word was a Japanese word meaning continuous and incremental improvement. What I didn't know was the degree to which it guided everything at Toyota.

As person after person at Toyota used "kaizen" in regular conversations, I asked more and more about it. Essentially, the practical concept of continuously and incrementally improving every part of Toyota's delivery of value to customers permeates every aspect of the organization. The reason I call Toyota one of the most commonsense companies in the world is because this concept of kaizen is how every company operates in the beginning.

A new company is formed to deliver value to customers. It struggles to find those customers. It earns some revenues and then struggles to find more customers. So it improves what it has to offer, which leads to more customers. After a few rounds of that cycle, many companies hit a comfort zone, a status quo, and then they operate within that status quo until a major crisis occurs, which stirs the cycle all over again.

At Toyota, the approach is to always maintain the attitude of being a new company, the attitude that says, "If we want to attract new customers and keep our current customers, we better deliver better value." No matter how successful they have become, Toyota continues to search for ways to add more value to customers.

Toyota first made cars for consumers in America in 1957. They flopped badly and sold only a few thousand cars. The Japanese engineers were used to making cars for Japanese highways, not American highways. Consequently, the engines overheated and the tires melted. However, Toyota persevered throughout the 1960s and 1970s and their cars gained a great deal of respect in the United States during the 1980s because of their quality and fuel efficiency. Toyota went on to become one of the largest and by far the most profitable automakers in the world.

Matthew May, in his book *The Elegant Solution: Toyota's Formula for Mastering Innovation*, wrote, "The Toyota organization implements a million ideas a year. It's fact. One million seems like an impossible target if you're talking about business ideas. But it's not, at least not for Toyota. It's the reason they're one of the planet's ten most profitable companies. It's why they make well over twice as much money as any other carmaker. It's the greatest source of their competitive advantage and staying power. It's their engine of innovation."[16]

Innovation is so important to building brand equity and winning the Management 500 that the entire next chapter is focused on it.

Win

What do Jeff Gordon, Richard Petty, Bobby Unser, Michael Schumacher, and Dale Earnhardt Sr. all have in common? They all built great brand equity for themselves and their racing teams. Yes, that's true, but they had one more thing in common. They all won a lot of races. None of them would have been nearly so successful in gaining sponsors and endorsements if they had not won consistently.

All of the thousands of autographs Richard Petty gave enhanced his brand, but they didn't make his brand of being The King. That was built through the 200 NASCAR races he won. Jeff Gordon's good looks and Dale Earnhardt Sr.'s intimidating driving style helped their brands, but the eleven NASCAR Winston Cups they won built the foundation for their massive earnings in sponsorships and endorsements.

Bobby Unser felt there were three steps to building a winning race team: go fast, lead, and win.[17] He explained this to mean when a new racing team comes together their first goal should be to get the car to go fast, their second goal should be to get the car to lead at least some of the laps during the race, and their final goal should be to win the race.

The same is true for your business. Working hard to recruit the best players, clarifying your customer value category, and getting the word to spread about your products and services are all important activities. That is how you go fast and occasionally take the lead.

However, if you want to generate significant, sustainable, and profitable growth for three consecutive years, your organization has to win and that means being the first or second choice of potential buyers for your products and services in the customer value category you've selected. It's not enough to persevere. You have to constantly improve and make the countless small decisions necessary to win. I'll come back to this topic again and again in Chapters 10, 11, and 12.

HOW DO YOU DAMAGE BRAND EQUITY?

You just spent several pages reading about how to build brand equity. Here are a few paragraphs on how to ruin it. It may have taken decades to build up your brand equity, but you can damage it very quickly.

Step one, break your brand promise. Your organization made a commitment to provide a certain type of value through the products and services it sells. You can break that promise intentionally or unintentionally, on a company-wide basis or an individual basis, but no matter how you do it you will lose brand equity whenever it happens.

If you promised speed and convenience and your products regularly show up late and damaged, you can kiss brand equity goodbye. If you promised long-term reliability of your products and then cut corners on quality to preserve cash flow, you may be saving dimes and losing dollars, a lot of them.

I had breakfast with a variety of business leaders one time, and one of them bragged on and on about his brand. He was the regional vice-president for a national professional services firm and said his firm was clearly the best in the industry. Over the next six months, several scandals emerged with members of his organization around the country in making up numbers for their clients in order to succeed. Finally, his firm collapsed because so many long-term customers simply walked away and took their business to the competition.

I had another breakfast with a number of business leaders and this man was present. He went on and on about how it wasn't fair that he had lost his job because he hadn't done anything wrong. He missed the big picture about brand equity. Whether the brand promise is broken at the top of an organization, at the bottom, or somewhere in between, if it's broken badly enough and often enough, the equity in the brand drops to zero.

The other way to damage brand equity is to stop improving. Just because your organization was the number-one choice for buyers in that customer value category three years ago, it doesn't mean they still feel that way today. Customers want the best possible value that is available today, not yesterday. The seven steps I outlined on how to build brand equity make up a dynamic process, not a static one. You don't apply them once and then stop. You apply them over and over again in order to continually strengthen the equity in your brand.

NASCAR'S PIT ROW: A CASE STUDY IN THE ART OF BRANDING

I was able to immerse myself for ten hours in the culture of NASCAR at the 2008 Sprint Cup Series LifeLock.com 400 at the Chicagoland Speedway. One of the highlights of the day was being allowed to spend forty-five minutes walking up and down pit row a few hours before the race started.

Pit row has the forty-three pit stalls that the drivers use during the actual race to have their tires replaced, cars refueled, and any car problems fixed. The actual racecars were sitting about twenty-five feet away on pit row itself. At each pit stop, the crew members were there to answer questions. There were several hundred fans walking up and down from one pit stop to another. Each pit stop had the corporate logos of the various sponsors for that specific racing team. There were well over 100 corporate logos including businesses from every conceivable industry on the walls of the pit stops and on the infield grass inside the track.

This was branding heaven, where customers, corporations, and racing teams all met in one spot. It created an extraordinary win-win-win situation.

The racing teams provided additional value to the customers by letting them see up close where the cars went during the race. I saw hundreds of photos being taken where fans would sit with the crew members and get their pictures taken in the pit stalls. Meanwhile, the drivers were spending time at a wide variety of locations so the fans could get close to them. This helped to build brand loyalty to NASCAR, the racing teams, and the individual drivers.

Every one of those pictures the fans took had corporate logos in them. That meant the sponsors would be seen thousands of times when those pictures were developed and shown with pride to family members and friends. These corporate sponsors weren't just hidden on the last page of a brochure. They were part of the fan interaction with the racing teams at the pit stalls. Because of this amazing synergy, the fans had a great time, the sponsors gained tremendous recognition, and the racing teams and the drivers earned fantastic revenues.

As I watched all of this several questions popped into my mind. Can you imagine professional baseball or football players letting fans look in their lockers a few hours before the game and have their pictures taken standing in front of those lockers? Or can you imagine corporate logos all over the lockers and the field itself? You might think that would ruin those games, and you might be right. However, think of the total cost of going to a major league baseball game or an NFL game. At the NASCAR event, the parking was free, the food was reasonable, and the ticket prices were not exorbitant.

More important, what does this have to do with your business?

Make a list of all of the types of customers you have. Now make a list of all the companies that would like to sell to those customers. Could you create a unique event for your customers featuring your products and services? Could you then include other companies at that event who could underwrite the costs and benefit from being in front of your customers? By creating this intersection of value for everyone involved, you may be able to strengthen your brand and the sustainable, profitable growth of your organization.

I encourage you to go to a NASCAR race, but get there way, way before it starts and let the lessons on branding soak in.

CHAPTER *TEN*

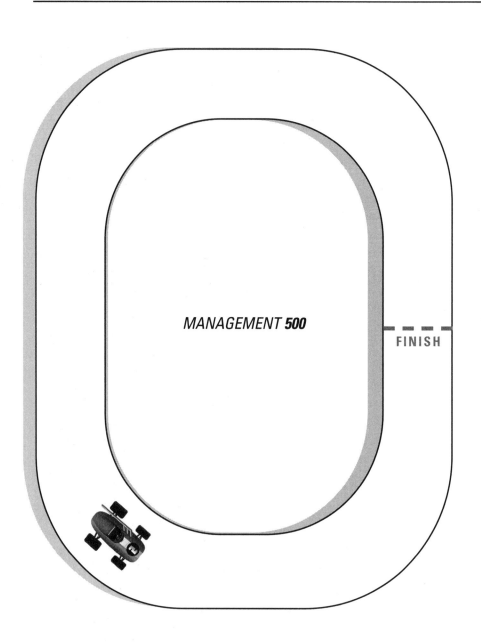

MANAGEMENT *500*

FINISH

INNOVATE TO
ACCELERATE

A business innovation is the creation of additional value that potential buyers will want to have and will pay for at a profitable margin to the organization. Both components are important: it has to be of greater value to the customers than what they already can purchase, and it has to be ultimately profitable to the organization that created it.

The most important word in the process of innovating is the word "no." In May 2006, BMW ran one of my all-time favorite ads in *Automobile Magazine*. On one page, in a large, bold font, it simply had the word, "No." On the next page, it essentially explained that BMW said no to compromising on a lot of good ideas, and instead said yes to focusing on a few great ideas that will hopefully make even better ultimate driving machines.

I love the advice in that ad for two reasons. First, BMW operates in a very genuine manner with that philosophy. Its ability to say no has allowed it to maintain its authenticity as the maker of great, sporty cars that perform exceptionally well. Second, and more importantly, it applies directly to every other business. If you want to achieve greatness as an organization and win the Management 500, you need to say no to a lot of good ideas so you can say yes to a few great ideas that will move your business forward.

If your plate and the plates of everyone in your organization are already full and you place three really important activities on the top of everyone's plates, then all you end up doing is diluting the impact of all of the activities. You need the courage to say no to a lot of good activities in order to say yes to the few activities that will matter the most.

Steve Jobs said, "People think focus means saying yes to the thing you've got to focus on. But that's not what it means at all. It means saying no to the 100 other good ideas that there are. You have to pick carefully. I'm actually as proud of many of the things we haven't done as the things we have done. We don't get a chance to do that many things, and every one should be really excellent."[1]

When Steve Jobs came back to Apple, Inc. as the interim CEO in 1997, Apple was selling something like eighty different computer models and variations, and they were eroding their profit margins. In 1998, Jobs said, "We sell consumer products and professionally oriented products. We need a desktop offering and a portable offering in each of those two categories."[2]

With this two-by-two approach to the market and by focusing on just four product platforms, Apple created the Power Mac G3, the PowerBook G3, the iMac, and the iBook. Those four products began to create positive momentum for Apple. By maintaining this extraordinary focus, Apple was able to add very few new products over the next ten years, but to do them extraordinarily well, as evidenced by the iPod and the iPhone. At Apple, focus is a business strategy, an approach that guides their wildly successful innovations.

Walt Disney used that same fanatical concentration in building a wide array of successful innovations. He personally focused on a few key projects at a time, and only after they were completed did he move on to a different project and let others maintain the earlier works. He maintained extraordinary focus on *Snow White and the Seven Dwarfs* from 1933–1937, but he let other people focus on animated films when he was concentrating on creating the Disneyland theme park in the early 1950s.[3]

Notice that innovation comes down to two rather ordinary concepts: concentration and the ability to stay focused. Rather than doing two dozen projects in the hopes that one of them will turn out to be a breakthrough, I encourage you to do just the opposite. Display the courage necessary to carefully select two or three projects and maintain the focus of your organization on creating as much value for your customers as possible within those projects.

Also, notice that truly innovative managers like Steve Jobs and Walt Disney don't just stay with a single product forever. Once they create tremendous value for customers in one area, they shift their focus to another area. Here is a critical difference between their approach and the approach of many other business managers. Jobs and Disney focused on very few projects at a time and over a period of thirty years each person created a wide variety of extraordinary innovations. Many managers focus on twelve projects at a time and end up with no extraordinary innovations over a period of thirty years.

THE OVERTAKE BUTTON

In an Indy-style racecar, there is a special button called "the overtake button."[4] During a race when a driver needs to pass another car he or she can push the overtake button, which gives the engine more fuel and the car more horsepower. This is a beautiful analogy of the power of business innovation.

A true business innovation is the overtake button that you can push as a manager to pass the competition. You always have it available to you, and it is important to use it on a consistent basis. However, if a racecar driver pushes the overtake button too often, the engine could become flooded with fuel and rendered ineffective. The same is true in your organization. If you try to create too many innovations simultaneously, you can overwhelm your organization and render it ineffective. Part of the art of business innovation is in finding the right balance of creating just enough innovations to win the race.

Say No Early and Often

When I hear that a work group is focused on creating a new innovation, I'm often stunned when I see their schedule. The members are spending the vast majority of their time on things not related to that specific idea. They are attending department head meetings and other

The Process for Innovating to Accelerate

1. Say no early and often.
2. Clarify a customer value challenge.
3. Organize your talent based on strengths, passions, and values.
4. Search for understanding.
5. Ignite conversations.
6. Move the idea forward.
7. Test small and dream big.

project meetings, interviewing potential employees, trying to solve crises as they arise, working with potential customers to gain new business, trying to win more business with current customers, spending countless hours checking e-mail and voicemail, and doing a host of other activities that have nothing to do with the innovation they are supposed to be producing.

Then, invariably, they wonder why they haven't made very much progress in the area of innovation. The reason they failed wasn't because of a lack of talent or work ethic. They simply didn't invest enough time or concentrated attention on the one area they wanted to improve for customers. You can generate extraordinary value for your customers, but you have to preserve your time and energy and the time and energy of your employees in order to place it on the innovation you want created.

As the head of the organization or the work group, you get to set a very important tone around the topic of focus. If you say yes to every meeting, every dinner invitation, every board membership, every golf tournament, every customer inquiry, and every demand your boss has, then you set the tone that everyone in the organization should run from one task to another without ever pausing to reflect on its relative importance. On the other hand, if you clearly demonstrate the ability to say no to a lot of good ideas so that you can say yes to a few great ideas, then other people will catch on that this is the way to improve results.

Make a list of all the things you and the other members of your organization are no longer going to do. Post this "No List" where everyone can see it. Get the members of your organization to take pride in not only saying no to activities, but, more importantly, in actually not doing them. Every two weeks check your No List and see to what degree you have actually stopped doing those things.

Here are some suggested items for your No List.

- No more meetings where attendees simply read an update to each other.

- No more days filled with meetings from 8 AM to 5 PM. (Instead, set a time limit of say three hours a day for meetings. You can select whatever number you want. My experience is people tend to fill the canister they've been given. If three hours a day is all any employee is allowed to be in meetings, how would that affect the behavior going into and during the meetings in your organization?)

- No more sending multiple e-mails or voicemails to folks who are not directly involved in a project. (Instead devise a regular update mechanism that folks can visit when they want to get an update.)

- No more nonstop open-door policy. (Instead have posted hours when you will be available for employees to run things by you, and then keep those hours open for your employees. Planning for requests of your time is far more effective than allowing a nonstop stream of immediate requests.)

The reason I put "saying no early and often" as the first step in the innovation process is based on observed behavior. The vast majority of managers I've observed fall into the "strong performer" category. These strong performers share a few things in common, and one of those things is a propensity to say yes to meetings and projects. Invariably they run from one meeting to the next and almost always are running in about fifteen minutes behind the start of the meeting. They pour sixty to seventy hours a week into their work and frequently say they have so much more that they want to get done.

Then there is a much smaller group of managers who are in the "extraordinary performer" category. These managers only attend a few meetings each day at the most. They are always on time and prepared for the discussion. They never seem rushed or chaotic in any way. When I ask them what they are working on, they invariably say, "Just a few things." When they are in a group meeting or an individual conversation, they are focused on what the other person is saying. They stay calm during the interaction, and respond with insightful comments.

Take out a sheet of paper. Before you focus on your whole organizations or on other individuals, start with yourself. Write down the single most important business outcome you want to improve. Then write down the three things you personally can do that would have the greatest positive impact on improving that outcome. Then flip the sheet over and write down a list of all the things you need to stop doing or spend a lot less time doing. Make sure your own No List is at least twice as long as your Yes List.

Clarify a Customer Value Challenge

Once you've honed your ability to say no to the vast majority of options available to you, you now have to say yes, in a very emphatic way, to something. Sometimes customers are very clear about what they want in terms of value, and sometimes they have no idea what they want. Both of those situations create opportunities for innovation.

Clarifying a specific value that you want to improve for your customers creates an inspiring challenge for your employees. It's the starting point for actually bringing a true business innovation to life. Innovation is not about building cool stuff. It is about building cool stuff that delivers additional value to customers who are willing to pay for the extra value. That's what makes it cool.

Toyota is one of the companies that truly epitomizes how to win the Management 500 through the power of innovation. In *The Elegant Solution: Toyota's Formula for Mastering Innovation*, Matthew May wrote, "Toyota pursues perfection by starting with the ideal, then working backward, removing anything that stands in the way. That means looking at the target in a fundamentally different way. It means asking 'What's blocking perfection?' instead of 'What can we improve?' The best way to bring it to life in a meaningful way is through the compelling story of Lexus. The mission was impossible: beat BMW and Mercedes-Benz at their own game. That meant besting both in comfort, styling, performance, handling, noise, aerodynamics, weight, and fuel efficiency."[5]

The challenge to build the best car in the world came from Eiji Toyoda, the Toyota Chairman, in 1983. The Lexus LS400 first went on the market on September 1, 1989, and it met every customer value challenge that had been set for it in 1983. That's how to innovate to accelerate.

I asked Lee White how his organization works to improve the performance of the Toyota racecars after the end of one year's racing season and before the beginning of the next season. His response was immediate:

> Dan, it's not like that at all. It doesn't spread out year to year. We're constantly working to improve our product. We don't wait until the end of the year to figure out how to get better for the next season. For us, finding ways to improve is a fifty-two-week, seven-day a week process that never stops.
>
> We're a racing company. We rarely stop working, and we definitely never stop thinking. No matter how good the racecar is and no matter how much our teams win, we always seek ways to help them improve. This process is almost identical to the ideological process of kaizen, which is a fundamental part of the Toyota Production System worldwide and means "constant improvement."[6]

Think about the great innovations in history. What customer value challenge did they meet? The automobile, particularly when Henry Ford made it affordable, democratized travel and reduced travel time dramatically. Henry Ford's innovative contribution was not in making a car. That had already occurred. The problem was that cars were incredibly expensive. His innovation was the assembly line that made it possible to make a lot of low-cost cars. The telephone increased the speed of communication, and replaced the telegraph that delivered communication, but in a much slower manner. E-mail increased the speed of delivering the written note. iPods made it possible for consumers to carry their music collection with them while making sure the musical artists got paid.

Before you start brainstorming about product or service innovations, start by clarifying the improved or completely new customer value that you want to deliver. Again, this takes time and if you fill up your day with meetings and e-mails you won't have the time to clarify a great customer value challenge.

These customer value insights don't need to come from you or any member of your executive team. As Matthew May wrote about applied creativity, "It's NOT sitting around dreaming up earth-shattering ideas behind closed doors, trying to be clever and creative in concocting a new secret sauce that will blow the doors off the competition. It's NOT a bevy of high-ranking executive managers involved in a costly and complex process engineered to boil the ocean. It is a frontline worker exploring, finding, and solving an important problem hands-on, down where the action is."[7]

Some innovations are small and some are large, but they are all important and all begin with the same question: "What would constitute greater value for our customers?" Is the customer value challenge that you want your organization focused on so precisely clear that it will cause people to think and act in ways that will generate extraordinary results? Don't worry about changing the world, worry about clarifying the improved condition you want potential buyers to experience from your products and services.

Organize Your Talent Based on Strengths, Passions, and Values

Once you have clarified the value for customers that you want to dramatically improve, the next step is to select the individuals who will be working on the project and organize them into certain roles and responsibilities. The key is to place your "A-players" on your most important innovations. If your organization maintains a very tight focus and only goes after one or two innovations at a time, you can always have A-players on every project.

Obviously an A-player for one project may not be an A-player on another project. Here are three questions to keep in mind as you organize the talent you want working on a particular innovation:

- Does the individual have the strengths to do his or her role at a very high level?

- Does the individual have passion for this particular customer value?

- Does the individual have the ability to work well with other group members on the long road ahead to creating a successful innovation?

If you don't get three yeses, I suggest you keep searching.

There are two models for assembling the members of an innovation team, and they both come from the world of filmmaking. The first approach is to craft the concept of the film you want to make and then reach out on a project basis to find the producer, director, writers, actors, editors, and so on who will work together to make that film. All of the individuals are under contract for that particular film. They all operate as free agents and separate after the film is completed.

For example, I encourage you to purchase *The Adventures of Indiana Jones: The Complete DVD Movie Collection*, which was made in 2003 before the fourth Indiana Jones movie was made. In addition to the first three Indiana Jones movies, there is a fourth DVD in this collection, and it's the one that has the greatest magic. The fourth DVD is called *Bonus Material*, and it has interviews with George Lucas, Steven Spielberg, Harrison Ford, and many others.

Recall the definition of innovation from the beginning of this chapter: the creation of additional value that potential buyers will want to have and will pay for at a profitable margin to the organization. What innovation did George Lucas and Steven Spielberg create? They took the basic concept of a comic-book hero and kept searching for ways to enrich the character, the story, the adventure, the humor, and the drama. The first three Indiana Jones films generated $1.2 billion in worldwide box office revenue. The fourth Indiana Jones film was created in 2008, nineteen years after the third film. That film alone, according to Wikipedia, generated $783,266,513 in worldwide box office revenue. I would call Indiana Jones a great business innovation.

I wish you could sit right next to me and watch this DVD on the making of the first three films in the series. There are so many lessons to be learned about innovation. The concept of the Indiana Jones movies was to create three live-action films about a comic book type of hero who always comes close to winning but always falls short to a certain degree.

One of the most powerful lessons from this DVD is the amount of creative effort Lucas and Spielberg poured into selecting each member of the cast and crew after the concept had been clarified. Every individual was discussed thoroughly for the part he or she would perform either in front of or behind the camera. In the end, this team, which was assembled after the concept for the film was clarified, achieved amazing results. The Indiana Jones movies became classics that are still being watched decades after they were originally made.

Is this an approach that your organization can use effectively? Can you reach out and bring together a group of individuals from outside of your organization to work together to meet a specific customer value challenge? It may not be feasible for you to have all the talent you need on a permanent basis inside your organization. By assembling talent to create a highly innovative product or service and then letting those free agents go to whatever organization they want to join, you may have a cost-effective method for generating great results.

The other model for assembling an innovation team is to select the members from within your current roster of employees. This is what I call "the Pixar approach" to filmmaking. At Pixar, full-time employees within the organization work on different film projects. These employees are developed at Pixar and are then selected to work on specific films based on their strengths and passions.[8]

As you look at the customer value challenge you want to address, how would you assemble some of your current employees into the best possible team for meeting that challenge? Rather than looking for outside expertise, how can you optimize the talent inside your organization and let your employees know that you believe in their ability to succeed?

Of course, a third option is available as well. In this approach, you combine the talents of full-time employees with temporary hires who join the team on a contract basis to create the innovative product or service. In this situation, the key is to create true teamwork throughout the group, regardless of whether the members are long-term employees or short-term hires. For the time being, everybody is a member of the group and plays an important role in creating the desired customer value.

Search for Understanding

Once you've decided on the customer value you want to create, the key is to get the team members that are working on that innovation to immerse themselves in better understanding the customer's situation. This may or may not include you. Don't feel that you have to be actively involved in the development of every innovation.

Two of my favorite books on innovation are *The Art of Innovation* and *The Ten Faces of Innovation* by Tom Kelley with Jonathan Littman. Tom Kelley is the general manager of IDEO, the world's largest design consultancy specializing in product development and innovation. IDEO has won countless awards for their innovative designs ranging from computers to toothbrushes.

In *The Art of Innovation*, Kelley wrote:

> We're big advocates of a principle we call "being left-handed,"
> developing empathy for consumers' needs, even if those consumers
> are very different from yourself. By studying people of all ages,
> shapes, cultures, and sizes we've learned that the best products
> embrace people's differences. Take kids, for instance. We prefer get-
> ting kids down on the test track, and watching them take prototypes
> out for a spin. Take something as basic as a toothbrush. On a project
> for Oral-B, we put brushes in the hands of young kids and quickly
> noticed the "fist phenomenon." Little kids grip the brush with their
> whole fist, unlike older kids, who use their fingertips. So we made a
> fat, soft, squishy grip that would be easy for them to handle.[9]

In *The Ten Faces of Innovation*, Kelley wrote about the importance of approaching innovation like an anthropologist. He explained a concept known as "Vuja De." He wrote, "Everyone knows that feeling of déjà vu, a strong sense that you have seen or experienced something before, even if you never really have. Vuja De is the opposite—a sense of seeing something for the first time, even if you have actually witnessed it many times before."[10]

If you want to really create a powerful business innovation, invest the time and energy it takes to really understand the potential buyer's situation. What excites and what frustrates him or her about the current experience? What will make the experience faster, smoother, more comfortable, more inspiring, more enjoyable, or better in some way that really matters to the buyer? Immerse yourself in the person's experience to gain the type of insights you need to dramatically improve that experience.

If you want to build a great racecar, observe cars in action, talk with drivers, and study the overall experience of what makes the cars go faster and with greater control. Enzo Ferrari wrote, "If a designer wants to produce a really great car, the best one possible, what he needs first of all are the suggestions of the best driver."[11]

If you want to build a more innovative product or service, observe customers, talk with them, and study their overall experience. Search for understanding as to what constitutes real value for these customers and what would constitute more value for them. Make sure you're not making up your answers in a board room, but rather from actual study of what customers go through.

Ignite Conversations

All the pieces are in place for the magic of innovation to occur. You have eliminated a host of activities that ate up people's time and energy. You have selected the customer value challenge to be sought after. You have assembled the team. You and/or the members of the team have searched for a deeper understanding of the overall customer situation relative to the value you want to create. Now it's time to innovate and actually create additional value that customers will want and will pay for at a profitable margin to your organization.

The starting point of additional value is an idea. Every innovative product or service begins with an idea and moves forward into reality as the result of a series of ideas.

Question: Where do those ideas come from?

Answer: Ordinary, old-fashioned conversations.

When you let the members of your innovation team simply discuss what they are learning and thinking, new ideas are formed for improving the value to the customer. The key is to realize the precious value of each idea. Each one has the capacity to play a critically important role in creating the breakthrough innovative product or service.

Not every idea will make it to the final cut, nor will every idea contribute value to the final version. But every idea has the potential to make a big contribution. If you dismiss an idea just because it came from a young or new member of the team, you may very well lose out on the combination of ideas that would have made a huge difference.

In the making of the film, *Raiders of the Lost Ark*, which is the first Indiana Jones movie, ideas for scenes came from conversations between George Lucas and Steven Spielberg, between actors, and between actors and Spielberg. The whole process was very collaborative, and collaboration is a critical element in innovation. You don't just want to assemble talented, passionate individuals who sit in vacuums. You want them to talk with each other, get to know each other, and be comfortable in exchanging ideas and building off each other's ideas.

Whether you assemble your team from a pool of long-term employees or bring in all the members from the outside or a combination of the two, it's very important to get them talking with each other about their ideas. You can ask a few open-ended questions like, "What do you think is the best way to deliver this value to customers?" or "What do you think we can do to improve the speed of delivery of value to customers?"

By asking an open-ended question, you're prompting the members of the team to throw their ideas on the table. The way you handle the next few minutes is very important. If you cut people off and reject their ideas, then you've doused their enthusiasm. On the other hand, if you just say, "Great idea" no matter what the person says, you lose credibility.

However, if you patiently listen to the idea in its entirety and then ask a follow-up question like, "How do you see that idea working with some of the other ideas we've heard today?," you set the tone for real collaboration to emerge.

Like watching a campfire grow from burning twigs underneath the logs, watch meaningful collaborations emerge by asking open-ended questions, listening attentively, and stepping back so others can step forward. In addition to your own behavior, compliment members of the team when you see the individuals asking good questions, listening well to others, and building on to ideas they've heard. In this manner, the innovation takes on a framework that can be attempted in real situations.

Move the Idea Forward

Innovation consists of creativity and grunt work. Creativity is the fun part. Crafting a customer value challenge and brainstorming with team members and customers to come up with ideas to meet that challenge is exciting. That's the no-pressure stage. Every idea tingles with possibilities, and every person is welcome to throw his or her ideas on the table. During a healthy collaborative conversation, the opportunities for success seem endless and a certain degree of euphoria sets in.

What separates the innovators from the dreamers is the act of continually moving ideas along until they become realities. This requires old-fashioned hard work. You won't move from initial idea to a truly innovative product or service in one giant leap. You'll get there with a thousand, or maybe two thousand, baby steps.

Matthew May wrote in *The Elegant Solution*, "The big earth-shattering ideas are few and far between. The real power of innovation lives in the minor tremors—the more plentiful and more immediately actionable smaller ideas. Most of the so-called revolutionary breakthroughs—the mythical eureka moments—are in reality smaller ideas combined, synthesized, and adapted to a new application."[12]

He wrote those words after eight years of teaching at the University of Toyota. His insights are based on hundreds of interactions with managers at Toyota. The sustained effort required to continually make incremental progress toward meeting the customer value challenge is what pulls many managers out of the race for achieving a powerful new innovation. You have to find the joy in making very small progress if you want to be able to hang in there all the way to completion.

In 1969 at the age of twenty-four, Ed Catmull had a new concept: to create a computer-animated feature-length film.[13] His vision was the exciting part of the work. The challenge was that in 1969 computers could barely manage to produce a still image, let alone a series of images that produced motion on the screen. In 1972, Catmull painstakingly produced a one-minute animated film about the movement of his left hand. Little by little, he developed more of the technology required to create a computer-animated film. His dream finally became a reality in 1995 with the creation of the first-ever computer-animated feature-length film: *Toy Story*.

Catmull, who became president of Disney/Pixar Animation Studios on May 5, 2006, provides a great example of the importance of gradually moving an idea forward. If he only focused on the end result of the feature-length film, he wouldn't have hung in there for twenty-six years. He saw progress in each step of the journey and realized how it could all ultimately lead to his dream.

As soon as members of your group come up with what they think is a good idea, encourage them to build a prototype of the idea. A prototype is a sketch or a simple model made out of whatever material is available to represent the idea. If you want to create a prototype for a service, which is intangible, you might encourage the team members to create a storyboard with drawings that explains how the service will flow for a customer. The value of the prototype is it helps the other members of the group to better understand how the idea might actually work for a customer.

One of my favorite chapters in the book *The Art of Innovation* is Chapter 6, "Prototyping Is the Shorthand of Innovation." Tom Kelley wrote, "Give your management team a report, and it's likely they won't be able to make a crisp decision. But a prototype is almost like a spokesperson for a particular point of view, crystallizing the group's feedback and keeping things moving. We believe in that great old saying, a picture is worth a thousand words. Only at IDEO, we've found that a good prototype is worth a thousand pictures."[14]

One thing great racecar teams and great management teams have in common is they embrace the iterative process of innovation. They know they will never create the final version of a car or a product or a service. Instead they realize that each race creates opportunities to find more ways to create value for customers.

Enzo Ferrari and his team built more than 131 prototypes of engines from 1946 to 1963. He felt races were useful because they stimulated technological progress. He said, "All the innovations learned from racing experience can find practical application in the normal production models in a relatively short period of time. To my successor I bequeath a simple inheritance: to keep alive that constant striving after progress that was pursued in the past."[15]

What ideas for creating more value for your customers are moving forward in your organization? Are the members of your team digging into the details of the ideas, creating prototypes so everyone can see the ideas in an early stage, and offering input that might make the ideas even better? This is the type of work it takes to move the ideas forward.

Test Small and Dream Big

Racecar drivers do three things with their cars: test, qualify, and race. Of the three, testing provides the best opportunities for innovation. During a test run, the racecar team can simulate various situations and then see what option produces the best results. Bobby and Al Unser, both winners of the Indianapolis 500, each had their own test track in Albuquerque, New Mexico. Bobby Unser wrote:

> Realistically, I might have tested more tires than any person dead or alive. Tires were the major key to more speed. Of course, tires weren't the only part of the car. Other components were tested and developed, such as new chassis setups, spark plugs, piston rings, and aerodynamics. Checking how things work was the only way to see if

any ideas were right, or if it was true in certain conditions. The objective was to win races, and anything that would gain an advantage in winning a race was well worth doing. I found testing was another way to gain an advantage, so I did a lot of it—and loved doing it."[16]

When your group has an idea ready for the marketplace, test it on a small basis no matter how excited everyone is about the revenue opportunities. It's far less expensive to give away 100 copies of a new product for actual customers to experience than it is to roll out 10,000 copies for sale that have a fault in them.

If you give away 100 copies, you can gather some valuable feedback on what is working well, what is not working well, and what would make the product more valuable for the customers. If you sell 10,000 copies of a hot new product and then find out all the problems with the product, you may hurt your reputation and your brand. That can cost your organization a great deal. The best time to make significant adjustments is during the test phase. Once the race for new sales begins, it may be too late to make major changes before the word gets out about the new product or service.

While the group is testing their new product or service on a small level, keep reminding them of the dream that lies in front of them. You and the rest of the group have set out to exceed a meaningful customer value challenge. This is the dream of how your team can make a huge difference in the lives of customers. Keep the group emotionally connected to the dream as they go through the hard work of incrementally improving the innovative product or service. Testing improves performance, but it is only sustained at peak levels if the team members are inspired to use their new knowledge to improve their creation.

SUMMARIZING INNOVATION

Limit yourself to the seven steps outlined in this chapter. Innovation is complicated enough without making it more so.

Say no to a lot of good ideas so you can really say yes to a few great ideas, clarify the customer value challenge you want to exceed, assemble the best team you can to beat that challenge, get the group to search for a strong understanding of the potential buyer's situation, ignite meaningful conversations among the team members, encourage the group to move ideas from concept to prototype to reality, and test the new product or service on a small scale before you roll it out on a major scale. And all the while keep the dream alive of what an incredible difference the innovation can make in the lives of other people.

CHAPTER **ELEVEN**

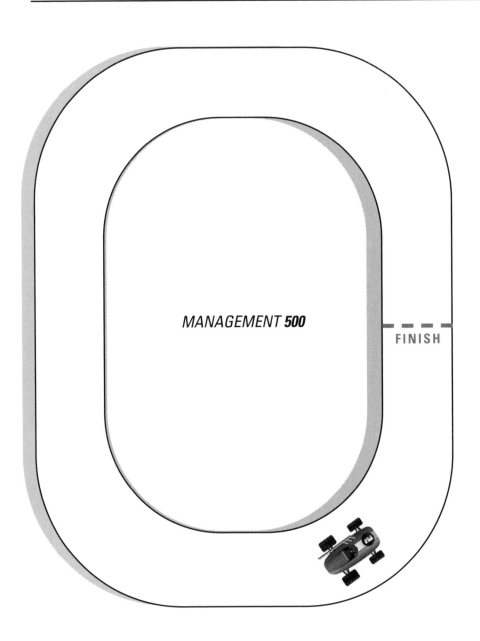

MANAGEMENT *500*

FINISH

PROGRESS THROUGH
TURNS IN THE TRACK

*"*Schumacher liked any car set up so that it turned into corners with vicious suddenness. Schumacher said, 'I think the main ability I have is a good and consistent feeling for the limit and I am able to run the car virtually a hundred percent on the limit. That's probably the difference in style.' He'd broaden that by explaining a driver might have the ability to do that in the entry of a corner but not, say, in mid-corner or at the exit again—or combinations of these. 'I can almost do this all the way around the corner,' said Schumacher.[1]*"*
—Christopher Hilton, in *Michael Schumacher: The Whole Story*

Up to this point in the book, every process and idea has been offered in the hope of improving your chances for winning the Management 500. However, preparing to win and actually winning are not the same things. In order to win, you have to deal with turns in your business situation and in the overall marketplace. Even though you expect them to happen at some point, you still have to guide your organization to make progress through those turns and not lose momentum or, even worse, crash.

In a car race, the best drivers separate themselves from the rest of the pack in the way they progress through turns in the track. This

ability is what separated Michael Schumacher, the seven-time Formula 1 Grand Prix World Champion, from the competition, and it is
what separated many of the other great drivers in history from the rest
of the pack. Just to get an idea of how important the skill of handling
the turns in the track is, here are a few statistics about race tracks to
keep in mind.

In the most famous IndyCar Series race, the Indianapolis 500, the
drivers face four turns per lap for 200 laps. That's 800 turns just to
complete the race, let alone win it. The Centurion Boats at the Glen is
a NASCAR Sprint Cup Series race held at Watkins Glen International
Raceway. The track has eleven turns and the drivers have to go ninety
laps. That's 990 turns the drivers have to make during that one race.
The Formula 1 Monaco Grand Prix has nineteen turns per lap and
consists of seventy-eight laps. That means the drivers make 1,482
turns going at roughly 200 mph.[2]

Do you see how important it is to make the most of every turn in
the race? If you're too slow, you'll be left behind; if you're too fast,
you may crash into the wall; and if you're too daring, you may end up
in a pileup or worse. It's during the race through the turns in the track
that the driver has to demonstrate tremendous skill, courage, timing,
and knowledge—all in a fraction of a second. Do you see why being
in great physical, mental, and emotional condition is extremely important to a driver's success?

Here's an attempt to put this in perspective. Imagine you're going
80 mph in the middle lane on the highway. That's pretty quick. Now
imagine a car passes you at 100 mph. You might think the person is
crazy. Now imagine another car doubles the speed of the first one and
goes 200 mph, and doesn't let you know until the last second whether
he or she is passing you on the right or the left. One last thing. Imagine all of this happens while you're driving through a 70-degree turn
in the highway. That's professional auto racing.

TURNS IN THE MANAGEMENT 500 TRACK

In management, a turn in the track is when the situation in front of
you suddenly changes. Keep in mind that mastering the art of progressing through turns in the track is as important to your success as a

business manager as it is for a racecar driver. Over the course of the next three years, you will face literally dozens and dozens of turns in the track. The way you handle these new situations will largely determine the success of your organization during that time.

Imagine you're stepping into a racecar in the Management 500 race, which has four turns per lap. Here are the turns you may encounter over the first four laps, and they are all based on real turns in the business track that I have watched business managers face. Just as a racecar driver is faced with multiple options at every turn to go high or low, speed up or slow down, and be defensive or offensive, you are also faced with multiple options at every turn.

Turn 1: A long-term employee who wanted the job you got threatens to ruin your reputation by twisting some of the words in a joke you told at a small meeting.

Do you send an e-mail to the entire organization and tell exactly what you said? Do you apologize for what may be construed as rudeness? Do you let the incident go, not say a word to anyone, and hope the situation doesn't turn into anything serious? You have options and every one of them has a potential upside and downside.

Turn 2: Your competitor comes out with an enormously popular new product that is gathering market share. You don't have this type of product anywhere in your planning for the next three years.

Do you drop some of your current projects to go after this hot new item and build a similar product? Do you stay the course with what you've been working on? Do you try to hire a key executive from the company that made the product to better understand what is happening in their organization? Do you pursue developing a different type of product that will shift the attention of customers back to your organization?

Turn 3: One of your best salespeople decides to leave the company.

Do you try to entice the person to stay with an extraordinary compensation package? Do you promote a person from within your organization to replace this individual? Do you reach outside the organization to bring in a completely different type of salesperson? Do you use this situation as an opportunity to revamp the sales department and shift into a different strategic approach to the marketplace?

Turn 4: Your organization is launching a new product and you are responsible for keeping your group focused on making this new product a success.

When you've seen the seventh presentation on this new product, do you stay engaged and ask good questions, or do you sit in the corner and check your Blackberry? I've seen this turn many times. When I asked an executive why he checked his messages during the product presentation, he said, "I've already seen that presentation many times. I've got other stuff to do." I replied, "If that's the case, then you need to leave the room because by sitting here you're sending the message to your employees that this new product is not important to you. Either pay attention to the presentation or leave."

If you're going to move successfully through this particular turn, you have to demonstrate that you see the extreme importance in this new product rollout.

Turn 5: A long-term customer whose purchases represent 38 percent of your revenue gives your organization thirty days' notice that he is moving to a different organization.

Do you fire hordes of employees? Do you shift employees to an all-out focus on gaining new clients? Do you focus on dramatically improving the quality of the value you offer to your current clients? How are you going to respond to this new scenario?

Turn 6: After months of pitching for a new client, you suddenly land a monster of a client that grows your business by 70 percent.

Do you ramp up hiring and risk lowering the consistent quality of what you deliver? Do you invest these new revenues in training and development? Do you take some of the focus off your current clients in order to meet the needs of this new client?

Turn 7: There are rumors on the street that your company is about to be bought by its main competitor.

Do you issue "No comment" releases to your employees and the media? Do you send out an e-mail explaining exactly what you know to all of your employees? Do you meet with just your senior leadership team and explain that your comments are to be kept confidential?

Turn 8: The long-term CEO of your organization retires suddenly.

As a business manager of one of the major divisions of the business, do you send the message that everything will remain status quo, or do you sit down with each employee and discuss how this change could affect his or her future?

Turn 9: Your business unit has been asked to test market a new service for your company.

Keep in mind that you're expected to deliver significant growth in both revenues and profits for the year. Do you jump up and say that you will be glad to do whatever it takes to support the new product test, or do you carefully consider it along with your business partners to determine if it really fits within your business plan for the year? If the test goes well, it might help your career, but if your actual business results are hurt because you lost focus due to the testing, you might hurt your career. What do you do?

Turn 10: You miss your profit goal by 15 percent for the quarter.

Do you toss out all the talk about improving teamwork and maintaining strategic focus, and just start firing employees and dropping costly projects in order to hit your profit projections for the next quarter? Do you admit that you made some mistakes, but that you believe in your employees and in your strategy and stay the course?

Turn 11: One of your department heads has an affair with an employee.

Do you meet with your head of HR and seek to fire the person immediately? Do you stay out of the way and let adults be responsible for their personal decisions? Do you discuss this situation with a variety of key individuals in your business? Do you confront the two individuals and tell them to stop seeing each other immediately?

Turn 12: Bad weather wipes out your organization's sales growth as compared to a year earlier.

Do you blame the poor results on the weather? Do you say that no matter what the organization has to make up for the losses before the end of the year? Do you make serious cuts in expenditures in order to regain momentum?

Turn 13: Customers reject the new business strategy and demand the old ways of doing business.

Do you toss out the new strategy and go back to the old way of creating and delivering value to customers? Do you persevere with the new direction and focus on educating customers as to why this new approach is better for them? Do you adjust the new strategy to be phased in over a number of years?

Turn 14: Two prominent members of your team can't stand being in the same room together and their feelings have bubbled over in key situations.

Do you sit the two of them down and let them know that they have to work things out? Do you fire one or both of them? Do you just let the situation go on and not say anything at all?

Turn 15: A new, very large competitor steps into the marketplace.

Do you revamp your business strategy in the face of this situation? Do you go on the offensive and market why your company is better than the other? Do you look to build a relationship with key executives at that business knowing you may be forced to close your business?

Turn 16: You get appointed a new boss who is truly overbearing and rude.

Do you just accept the rude behavior and not say anything? Do you make feisty comments back to the individual in front of other people? Do you meet with the person one-on-one to discuss observed behaviors where the person was rude to you and to other people?

That's just four laps in The Management 500. What else might happen during the next 196 laps? Each turn in the track comes at you so fast you won't have time to develop a new approach for every new situation.

Optimize Your Energy

Now that you've seen just sixteen possible turns in the Management 500 track do you realize even more the enormous importance of physical conditioning for a business manager? The vast majority of times I've seen managers crash and burn was when they were overextended and exhausted. Inevitably, they would later say they knew it was the wrong move to make, but they just wanted to get it over with.

In 1994, Michael Schumacher was injured for a month and missed four of the sixteen Formula 1 Grand Prix races. However, he used his injury time to increase his physical conditioning. He said, "I did six to eight hours everyday at 2,000 meters and it paid off. I felt really

---

The Process for Progressing through Turns in the Track

1. Optimize your energy.

2. Isolate your train of thought.

3. Stay calm and don't try too hard.

4. Know when to go fast and, more important, when to go slow.

5. Clarify your options quickly.

6. Be decisive.

7. Admit your mistakes, maintain humility, learn, and mature.

---

great."[3] Despite missing 25 percent of the races that year, Schumacher won his first world championship. His superior conditioning allowed him to be at his best when he needed to be.

You don't have to be a world-class athlete to be a great business manager, but the stronger your reservoir of energy the better your chances are of successfully handling the turns in the business track.

Isolate Your Train of Thought

Chris Hilton wrote, "The most aware human beings you're ever likely to meet are Formula 1 drivers and they prosper by isolating one train of thought from another train of thought."[4]

In order to handle a sudden new change in your professional situation, it's very important to focus on one item at a time. If a driver suddenly starts to think about a situation at home, he or she may lose concentration for two or three seconds and run into a concrete wall. At work, you may say something without thinking that costs you your job or a major new customer. Narrow your concentration to the turn you're facing at the moment. Maintain your attention on understanding what it is your dealing with.

Stay Calm and Don't Try Too Hard

Ultimately, this was the primary reason for Schumacher's success. He was able to stay calm and not overdrive his car in any situation. Ross Brawn, the chief tactician for the Ferrari Racing Team, said, "The other remarkable thing about Michael is when we talk on the radio it's like you and I having this conversation. It's a perfectly normal discussion. What I like about Michael is that even the most aggressive tactics from other drivers in normal racing never elicit a comment from him. He always has spare mental capacity when he's driving a car. When some of the drivers are at the limit they've got nothing left mentally or physically. Michael, you always feel, has a margin to think about things and take everything into consideration."[5]

The very best managers I've observed remained very calm in the midst of the worst turns. When their companies went through a downsizing, they pulled out a piece of paper and calmly wrote down step by step what they would do in the next few days for their employees and themselves. They didn't get overly emotional, but simply did what they could as well as they could do it.

The managers who usually produce the worst performances are those who simply try too hard. They try to make everyone happy, they try to improve every result, and they try to make every presentation perfect. Instead of creating a calm environment, they create total chaos. Stay calm, do your best, and see what happens.

Know When to Go Fast and, More Important, When to Go Slow

The best racecar drivers develop a sense of when to push the car past a competitor and when to avoid an unnecessary risk. This sense comes from one thing: experience. As you face turns in your business, pause for just a moment and ask yourself, "Should I move as fast as possible to resolve this situation or should I go slow and see if it takes care of itself?" You may make the wrong move, but by making it consciously you can then review it later to see what worked well and why it worked well and what did not work well and why it did not work well.

Clarify Your Options Quickly

Racecar drivers can't write down their thoughts while they are driving. That's why they have crew chiefs to communicate with. You, on the other hand, can take out a piece of paper in the midst of any situation and answer this question, "What are my options?" I've never seen a business situation where a manager didn't have options to choose from. Having options increases the sense that you are in control of your destiny. With options, you feel you get to make the choice.

Make your first response to any turn a compilation of your options. Once you see what you have to choose from, then you can make your move. If you jump into action first, you may miss out on a much better move.

Be Decisive

Once you choose your option, go with confidence. Be decisive. Few things frustrate employees more than a boss who constantly changes his or her mind. By staying calm in a stressful situation, carefully outlining your options, and moving with decisiveness, you instill a greater sense of confidence in your team members.

Michael Schumacher said, "I try to feel where the limit is at each corner. In order to detect the limit, I must however always try to drive faster than it seems the car can go. I want to exhaust the efficiency of the car completely, meet exactly the point where it performs best."[6]

You might make a move that produces poor results. That's OK. Unlike a racecar driver where the wrong decision can result in a crash, or much worse, you will always be able to live another day. The worst thing that can happen is you might lose your job. Sometimes even that turns out to be a positive turn in your career. Be decisive and go forward with courage. That's not an inspirational thought. That's a realistic management necessity.

Admit Your Mistakes, Maintain Humility, Learn, and Mature

In the end, this was Schumacher's legacy. When he crashed, he took responsibility. He said it was his fault and that he still had a lot to learn. Then he did one more thing. He matured as a driver. He learned to drive fast slowly.

In 1992, Schumacher said, "One thing I have learned is that I need to have a better overview of all situations and to have a bit more control of everything in the job. It is in this that I am inexperienced and I need to learn." Two years later he won his first Formula 1 Grand Prix World Championship. The next year he won his second world championship. And then he won five more from 2000–2004.

In my keynotes and seminars I've noticed a phenomenon that I call "The Life-Long Learner Approach." There is usually one person in the audience who leans forward more intensely than anyone else, engages more fully in conversations than anyone else, and is older than me. Invariably during a break I find out from other people that this person is by far the most successful person in the group and is vastly more successful than I am. However, he or she comes seeking insights to improve.

When I've spoken with these individuals, I always asked, "What were you hoping to get out of this meeting?" Invariably, the person says, "I wanted some ideas on how I can improve my performance and the performance of my organization." After these conversations, I always walk away more inspired to keep learning.

The great managers, the ones who win the Management 500, make decisions, admit when they made a mistake, always put the organization ahead of their own interests, learn something everyday, and continually mature into better managers.

OPERATING UNDER THE CAUTION FLAG

However, there is one turn in the track that has nothing to do with what's right in front of the racecar driver. It's the caution flag. When debris lands on the track or a car gets damaged while racing, the caution flag is waved and all the drivers have to slow down and get behind the pace car. That doesn't seem too bad, except for the lead driver. Even if the driver in front has a fifteen-car length lead, he or she has to slow down and let all the other cars line up right behind so the whole caravan of cars goes around the track at the same time. The lead that had been built over the course of the race has suddenly evaporated.

This same thing happens in business. You're doing a good job and staying focused. You've built tremendous momentum and you're well beyond the pace needed to achieve all of the important business outcomes. Your organization is by far the best in the industry, and you continually generate significant, sustainable, and profitable growth.

Then suddenly the marketplace changes. Instantly all the businesses in your industry are slowed way down. A series of national stories about your industry immediately sends even your most loyal customers searching for alternatives.

Think of the housing downturn that occurred in 2007 and 2008. Suddenly the most successful and the least successful real estate agents were compressed into an incredibly tight market. The leader's lead was no longer what it had been. When there is even an isolated incident of Mad Cow disease, it sends restaurants and grocery stores into a temporary spiral, whether they were way ahead of their plan or way behind.

This is why it is so important to focus on improving performance and not solely on your relative position compared to others at any given moment. Just because you had a great or terrible quarter doesn't mean you're stuck in that position forever. Perhaps your competitor made a big sale right before the quarter ended, and you made one right after the next quarter started. It looks like you're way behind when in reality you're not.

Markets change, trends change, and customers get fickle. Rather than letting a sudden change cause you to slow down or speed up your performance, focus on continually improving what you do. In this way, you are making progress through the turn because you're learning from the experience rather than giving up. You're maturing and preparing yourself for greater success in the future.

CHAPTER TWELVE

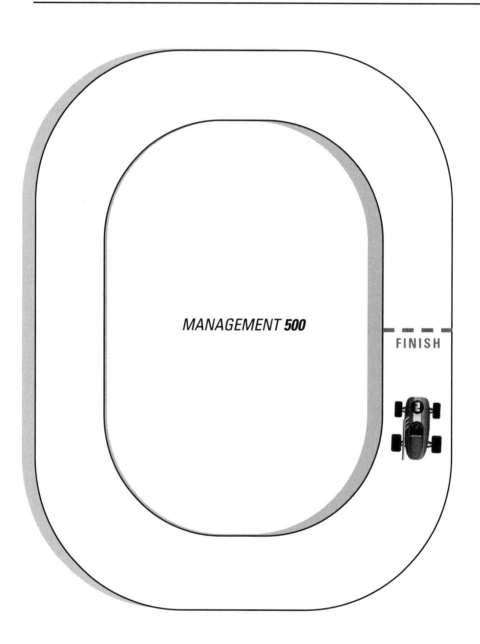

MANAGEMENT *500*

FINISH

FINISH WITH
FOCUS

The 1979 Daytona 500 was the first 500-mile race NASCAR ever had on live television from start to finish.[1] Donnie Allison was barely leading Cale Yarborough with one lap left in the race. All the other drivers were way behind. If Yarborough could complete a slingshot pass by pulling up directly behind Allison and then zip around him, he would win the race. When Allison went low, Yarborough hit him from behind and knocked both drivers out of the race. Richard Petty, who had been in a distant third position, flew through and grabbed the victory.

When I went to Chicago to experience my first NASCAR Sprint Cup series race, Jimmie Johnson, the two-time defending Sprint Cup Champion, had managed to take the lead from Kyle Busch with about sixteen laps to go in the 2008 LifeLock.com 400. He extended that lead to twenty car lengths going into the final two laps with just three miles left. A lot of people thought Johnson had the race won. Then the unexpected happened, and a caution flag came out. When the race resumed, Busch immediately got right behind Johnson, who tried to play defense. Johnson went low on the track, and Busch went high. With that move Kyle Busch stormed to victory.

The race isn't won until you cross the finish line in first place. In the Management 500 that means achieving three consecutive years of significant, sustainable, and profitable growth. However, there are a lot of important laps to complete during the three years. Before I get to those, here's the process to keep in mind.

The Process of Finishing with Focus

1. Define what "winning" means for each lap.

2. Maintain your concentration.

3. Go past the end.

Define What "Winning" Means for Each Lap

In order to win a lap, you have to know what that means. In car racing, that's easy. At the end of every lap it's obvious who is in first place. However, in business you have to define what success means for each lap. Achieving significant, sustainable, and profitable growth for three straight years means you've done pretty darn well. However, that's just the ultimate finish line after having successfully won a lot of laps around the track.

For every meeting, activity, and project you have determine in advance what a successful lap would be. A lot of mediocre performances don't add up to a win in the Management 500.

Maintain Your Concentration

Concentration in the midst of a race is the crucial factor. Losing sight of what needs to be done during each lap and not paying attention to the details can cause you to fall way behind. Know the end you want to reach for each lap, and then stay focused on crossing that line. Sometimes winning doesn't seem possible, but by maintaining your concentration and getting a few lucky breaks, you really can grab a victory. If you lose your concentration, however, the lucky breaks won't matter.

Go Past the End

Can you imagine a racecar stopping exactly at the finish line? Wouldn't that look silly? Racecars fly right across the finish line to win the checkered flag. Stay focused on winning each lap and then at the end of the three years fly across the ultimate finish line with confidence.

LAPS IN THE MANAGEMENT 500

Over the course of the next three years, you will establish and attempt to win multiple laps. If you put all of your energy and attention only into the ultimate goal of achieving three consecutive years of significant, sustainable, and profitable growth, you may very well miss out on achieving all of the items that add up to the overall victory.

Adrian Newey, the aerodynamicist and technical director for the McLaren Formula 1 Racing Team that won the 1998 and 1999 world championships, said:

> The process of designing the MP4/14 was not something started on one specific day as a blinding piece of technical inspiration. Like everything in Formula 1, it evolved and took shape as part of a process that involves building on all the knowledge and data that has cascaded down the year.
>
> One of the things that has changed dramatically in Formula 1 is the amount of development work that is carried out on a Grand Prix car during the course of the season. The big gains in performance tended to be made over the winter between seasons, but nowadays that development process continues throughout the year.[2]

My main point is that rather than starting up dozens of items that never get truly completed, focus on taking a few pieces all the way to the finish line. Then move to another item and drive it all the way to the finish line. Do that lap after lap and you will secure a victory.

What follows are suggestions and questions for you to consider regarding a variety of the laps involved in winning the Management 500. Consider my thoughts, but even more important, write down for yourself what you think the finish line looks like under each item. Then focus your attention on crossing that line successfully.

Relationships

In terms of your employees is it enough to just set up meetings with them? Or do you need to show up on time, listen attentively, and engage in a meaningful conversation? What about your customers, suppliers, and business partners? What is the finish line you're trying to cross in terms of relationships with each of these different groups of individuals?

E-Mails

As you're pounding out your replies to e-mails, what do you think the end of the lap looks like? Is it enough to just send the first thought that comes to your mind, or is it better to think through your response and remove any sarcasm or anger that it contains? If you're initiating a communication on e-mail, what is the end that you're trying to attain? Will your e-mail help to make that a reality or should you pick up the phone or meet in person?

Speeches

Many times I've seen executives invest countless hours in preparing a speech only to ruin its impact by making ill-advised off-the-cuff comments. Don't just focus on the actual speech. Concentrate instead on what the finish line looks like in terms of a successful speech. Does it include causing new behaviors or gathering support for a new initiative? How can you complete an effective lap in terms of delivering a successful speech unless you've clarified what defines that success?

Voicemails

If you're going to leave a voicemail for an individual or group, first decide your desired outcome. Then think through the voicemail and see if you believe it will achieve what you want. Many phone systems allow you to listen to your message before you send it. If yours has that capacity, you might want to use it if your message is important or complicated.

Strategy

At what point can you declare a business strategy a victory? Is it when the strategy appears in the company brochure? Is it when it has been communicated to all employees, suppliers, and business partners? Or when it affects decisions and behaviors of everyone involved with the organization in ways that generate better business outcomes? Rather than going for a false early lead, determine the factors that will declare a truly successful lap.

Plans

The implementation of a strategy only occurs when a planned activity is executed. So when is the plan a done deal? Is it when each department has completed their planning process and handed it in to you? Is it when the plans have been converted into actions? Is it when the actions have been assessed in terms of what worked well and what did not work well? You decide on the finish for the planning process. Just make sure it's a worthwhile finish to pursue.

Website

Is your website helping you to achieve a victory, a second-place finish, or a crash (no pun intended)? In my experience, too often a company rolls out a new website only to have frustrated customers calling about wrong numbers and the inability to order products on-line.

Advertising

What constitutes a successful advertising campaign? Is it having a clear message, is it getting good feedback from a focus group, or is it impacting customer behaviors? As you develop your marketing materials, keep in mind the line you want to cross as the result of your advertising efforts.

Meetings

Meetings certainly are the greatest time-consuming business device ever created. Whether in person or on a web conference, the same challenges occur. Is it meaningful or a waste of time? Don't just focus on the rules of meeting behavior. Concentrate also on what constitutes a successful meeting. What needs to occur during the course of any meeting, large or small, to be able to say it was a success? Clarify that so everyone in your organization knows at the end of any given meeting whether or not it was a successful lap toward the overall victory.

Racing just for the sake of racing without having a finish line holds no excitement for the fans or drivers. Holding meetings just for the sake of having them without a clear sense of what defines success holds no excitement for the attendees.

Finances

What financial indicators do you need to see to determine whether or not you are making progress toward winning the Management 500? Having an amazing quarter doesn't guarantee success if most of the revenue is coming from a one-time client. What makes a successful financial analysis? This is a very important lap to lead if you want to make wise decisions in the future for generating significant, sustainable, and profitable growth.

Markets

What do you need to know about trends in the marketplace in order to confidently make decisions impacting the future of your organization? There are no perfect crystal balls in business, but there are certain key pieces of information that can help you increase your chances for success. What would make up the ideal market research for your business?

Talent

There is a lot of talk these days about getting the right people in your organization. How will you know if you've successfully won in terms of attracting, retaining, and developing the right type of employees for your organization? It's not enough to talk about having great people or telling them how important they are to the organization. You need to know what defines a great lap in the area of talent management.

Media

What is your organization's relationship with the media like? Is it what you want it to be? How can you close the gap and build the type of relationship you want with the media and improve the way you're positioned by the media in the marketplace?

In NASCAR, many drivers go through extensive media training in order to communicate effectively with reporters. How do you want the members of your organization to come across in media situations?

Branding

You have a brand. That's a given. A brand is how customers and potential customers perceive the value they receive or would receive from your organization if they bought from it. However, do you have the brand you want? What would define a victorious lap for your organization in terms of its brand? Is it getting phone calls from customers, is it selling a particular type of product at record levels, or is it successfully letting go of specific services and replacing them with new services?

Innovation

The hype about innovation comes in waves and goes through cycles. Rather than waiting for it to become a buzzword again, write down what winning means in terms of new innovations. Is it enough just to have projects in the pipeline? Is it enough to replace older products with new ones so that your organization demonstrates a fresh face to the public? Or does the innovation need to have a certain impact in the marketplace in order to be called a success?

Culture

The whole concept of corporate culture seems so nebulous. How will you know if your employees have successfully created the culture you want? What are the indicators you're looking for? Do you need to demonstrate a connection between employee behaviors and business results?

Teamwork

For all the talk about teamwork, it doesn't seem to happen very often. If a team is a group of individuals who support one another toward achieving a meaningful purpose, how will you know when your group has won the teamwork lap? Teamwork will always remain in the realm of the intangible unless you make it tangible. Take the time to decide what determines success in the area of teamwork. You have to know what you're going after in order to create it.

Learning

I've never met a successful manager who didn't focus on learning. However, it's not enough just to read book after book after book and scan through the *Wall Street Journal* every day. Just as with all of the pieces of great management performance, professional development needs a well-defined statement of success. It's not that you're ever going to be finished learning—it's that you need a clear line in front of you that tells you what effective learning looks like. Decide that before you decide where to invest in learning experiences.

Leadership

Leadership is real and it's really important, but its success is not intuitively obvious. What needs to happen for you to be able to determine if you are winning as a leader? Is it just getting your way? Is it having employees telling you that you did a great job? Is it impacting behaviors throughout your organization that collectively impact key business results?

Take the time to write down what you believe needs to happen for you to consider your impact as a leader to be truly effective. Consider multiple areas including business results, the team you have assembled, the consistent behaviors of your employees, the clarity of the value your organization offers to customers, and so on. There are many different types of successful leaders so don't get caught up in having a certain type of personality or style. Focus instead on the tangible and intangible outcomes you want to generate as a leader.

Improvement

Constantly improving is a common point of emphasis throughout this book. However, it is possible to constantly improve and make no real progress. What types of improvements do you need to make as an individual and does your organization need to make as a whole in order to say you have won the lap in the area of improving? Just going to workshops doesn't constitute meaningful improvement. In your opinion, what does? Clarify what defines success in terms of improvement and work to win that lap.

THE FINISH LINES WITHIN THE FINISH LINE

The final key to winning the Management 500 is to focus all the way to the end of each lap that you will be competing in over the course of the next three years. Not only that, but you will have to win many of the same laps over and over again. You don't build great teamwork once and then be done with it. Nor do you conduct great market research or a sensational financial analysis just once. You need to win those races and all of the others we've discussed in this book over and over and over in order to win the Management 500.

Enjoy the race. It's an exciting adventure.

INTRODUCTION

1. NASCAR's primary race series is known as the NASCAR Sprint Cup Series. In the past it has been called the NASCAR Nextel Cup Series, NASCAR Winston Cup Series, and NASCAR Grand National series.
2. Christopher Hilton, *Michael Schumacher: The Whole Story* (Newbury Park, Calif.: Haynes Publishing, 2007), pp. 75, 88.

CHAPTER 1

1. Enzo Ferrari, *The Enzo Ferrari Story: An Autobiography* (New York: The MacMillan Company, 1964), p. 33.
2. Peter D'Epiro and Mary Desmond Pinkowish, *Sprezzatura: 50 Ways Italian Genius Shaped the World* (New York: Anchor Books, 2001), pp. 353–356.
3. Ferrari, p. 109.
4. Hilton, p. 18.
5. D'Epiro and Pinkowish, pp. 353–356.
6. Eric Clapton, *Clapton: The Autobiography* (New York: Broadway Books, 2007), p. 139.
7. Alan Henry, *McLaren Formula 1 Racing Team* (Newbury Park, Calif.: Haynes North America, Inc., 1999), p. 39.
8. Henry, p. 103.
9. Hilton, p. 34.
10. Steve Martin, *Born Standing Up: A Comic's Life* (New York: Scribner, 2007), p. 75.
11. Helen Garson, *Oprah Winfrey: A Biography* (Westport, Conn.: Greenwood Press, 2004), pp. xiii–xiv.
12. Neal Gabler, *Walt Disney: The Triumph of the American Imagination* (New York: Alfred A. Knopf, 2006), p. 222.
13. Robert Sellers, *Harrison Ford: A Biography* (London: Warner Books, 1993), p. 38.
14. Ibid., pp. 306–307.
15. Larry McReynolds with Jeff Honeycutt, *How to Become a Winning Crew Chief* (Phoenix, Ariz: David Bull Publishing, 2005), p. 11.
16. Ferrari, p. 32.
17. Hilton, p. 51.
18. Noel Tichy and Warren Bennis, *Judgment: How Winning Leaders Make Great Calls* (New York: Portfolio, 2007), pp. 22–23.
19. Peter Drucker, *The Effective Executive* (New York: Harper & Row, 1966).

CHAPTER 2

1. Larry McReynolds with Jeff Honeycutt, *How to Become a Winning Crew Chief* (Phoenix, Ariz.: David Bull Publishing, 2005), p. 137.

CHAPTER 3

1. Jeff Gordon with Steve Eubanks, *Jeff Gordon: Racing Back to the Front—My Memoir* (New York: Atria Books, 2003), p. 76.
2. Joe Gibbs, *Racing to Win* (Portland, Ore.: Multnomah, 2003).

CHAPTER 4

1. Leigh Montville, *At the Altar of Speed: The Fast Life and Tragic Death of Dale Earnhardt* (New York, Doubleday, 2001); Hilton; Gordon with Eubanks; Liz Clarke, *One Helluva Ride: How NASCAR Swept the Nation* (New York, Villard Books, 2008), pp. 27–28.
2. Leander Kahney, *Inside Steve's Brain* (New York: Portfolio, 2008), pp. 203–219.
3. Randall Stross, *The Wizard of Menlo Park: How Thomas Edison Invented the Modern World* (New York: Crown Publishers, 2007).

CHAPTER 5

1. Lee White, personal interview, August 2008.
2. Clarke, pp. 159–160.
3. Geoff Smith, personal interview, October 2008.
4. Charles Kepner and Ben Tregoe, *The New Rational Manager* (Princeton, N.J.: Kepner-Tregoe, Inc., 1981); Alan Weiss, Ph.D., *The Unofficial Guide™ to Power Managing* (Foster City, Calif.: IDG Books Worldwide, Inc., 2000).
5. Jeffrey Liker, *The Toyota Way: 14 Management Principles from the World's Greatest Manufacturer* (New York: McGraw-Hill, 2004), pp. 223–265.
6. Alan Greenspan, *The Age of Turbulence: Adventures in a New World* (New York: Penguin Press, 2007), p. 17.

CHAPTER 6

1. Bobby Unser with Paul Pease, *Winners are Driven: A Champion's Guide to Success in Business & Life* (Hoboken, N.J.: John Wiley & Sons, Inc., 2003), pp. 1–2.
2. Greenspan, p. 493.

CHAPTER 7

1. Gordon with Eubanks, pp. 73–74.
2. Ibid., pp. 223–235.

3. Jeffrey Liker and David Meier, *Toyota Talent: Developing Your People the Toyota Way* (New York: McGraw-Hill, 2007), p. 5.
4. Kahney, pp. 154.
5. Henry, pp. 15–25.
6. Liker and Meier, p. 22.
7. Ibid., p. 18.
8. Montville, p. 71.
9. Lee White, personal interview, August 2008.

CHAPTER 8

1. Gordon Kirby, "Before 'The Captain' Won His Pips," *Motor Sport* magazine, April 2008, pp. 62–68.
2. Mike O'Leary, *Mario Andretti: The Complete Record* (St. Paul, Minn.: MBI Publishing Company, 2002), pp. 7–20.
3. Benjamin B. Tregoe and John W. Zimmerman, *Top Management Strategy: What It Is and How to Make It Work* (New York: Touchstone Books, 1980); Robert S. Kaplan and David P. Norton, *The Strategy-Focused Organization: How Balanced Scorecard Companies Thrive in the New Business Environment* (Cambridge, Mass.: Harvard Business School Press, 2001); Andrew Grove, *Only the Paranoid Survive: How to Exploit the Crisis Points that Challenge Every Company* (New York: A Currency Book, 1996); W. Chan Kim and Renée Mauborgne, *Blue Ocean Strategy: How to Create Uncontested Market Space and Make the Competition Irrelevant* (Cambridge, Mass.: Harvard Business School Press, 2005).
4. Grove, pp. 3–4.
5. Clarke, pp. 124–125.
6. Montville, pp. 80–95.
7. Kahney, p. 185.
8. Gordon with Eubanks, p. 157.

CHAPTER 9

1. Geoff Smith, personal interview, October 2008.
2. Ed Laukes, personal interview, August 2008.
3. Hilton, p. 172.
4. Montville, p. 129.
5. Clarke, p. 139.
6. Ibid., pp. 154–173.
7. Nancy Roe Pimm, *Indy 500: The Inside Track* (Plain City, Ohio: Darby Creek Publishing, 2004), p. 43.
8. David Kiley, *Driven: Inside BMW, the Most Admired Car Company in the World* (Hoboken, N.J.: John Wiley & Sons, Inc., 2004), p. 111.
9. Montville, pp. 73, 81.
10. Al Ries and Jack Trout, *Positioning: The Battle for Your Mind* (New York: McGraw-Hill, 2001).
11. Gabler, pp. 213–215.
12. Malcolm Gladwell, *The Tipping Point: How Little Things Can Make a Big Difference* (New York: Little, Brown, and Company, 2000), pp. 7–9.
13. Gladwell, p. 34.

14. Kiley, p. 108.
15. Ibid., p. 123.
16. Matthew May, *The Elegant Solution: Toyota's Formula for Mastering Innovation* (New York: Free Press, 2007), pp. xi–xii.
17. Unser with Pease, p. 41.

CHAPTER 10

1. Betsy Morris, "What Makes Apple Golden," *Fortune*, March 17, 2008, p. 72.
2. Jeffrey Cruikshank, *The Apple Way: 12 Management Lessons from the World's Most Innovative Company* (New York: McGraw-Hill, 2006), pp. 22–23.
3. Gabler.
4. Pimm, p. 33.
5. May, pp. 42–43.
6. Lee White, personal interview, August 2008.
7. May, p. 18.
8. Kahney, pp. 110–115.
9. Tom Kelley with Jonathan Littman, *The Art of Innovation: Lessons in Creativity from IDEO America's Leading Design Firm* (New York: A Currency Book, 2001), pp. 33–34.
10. Kelley with Littman, *The Ten Faces of Innovation: IDEO's Strategies for Beating the Devil's Advocate & Driving Creativity Throughout Your Organization* (New York: Currency Doubleday, 2005), p. 18.
11. Ferrari, p. 84.
12. May, pp. 38–39.
13. David Price, *The Pixar Touch: The Making of a Company* (New York: Alfred A. Knopf, 2008), pp. 13–15.
14. Kelley with Littman, *The Art of Innovation*, p. 112.
15. Ferrari, pp. 32–33.
16. Unser with Pease, pp. 172–173.

CHAPTER 11

1. Hilton, p. 181.
2. www.nascar.com, www.formula1.com, www.indycar.com.
3. Hilton, p. 149.
4. Ibid., p. 143.
5. Ibid., pp. 276, 282.
6. Ibid., p. 246.

CHAPTER 12

1. Clarke, pp. 24–25.
2. Henry, pp. 120–121.

INDEX

235